How To Build **a Bobber On a Budget**

How To Build a Bobber On a Budget

Jose de Miguel

MOTORBOOKS

Quarto.com

First published in 2008 by Motorbooks, an imprint of The Quarto Group, 100 Cummings Center, Suite 265-D, Beverly, MA 01915, USA.
T (978) 282-9590 F (978) 283-2742

© 2008 Motorbooks

All rights reserved. With the exception of quoting brief passages for the purposes of review, no part of this publication may be reproduced without prior written permission from the Publisher.

The information in this book is true and complete to the best of our knowledge. All recommendations are made without any guarantee on the part of the author or Publisher, who also disclaim any liability incurred in connection with the use of this data or specific details.

We recognize, further, that some words, model names, and designations mentioned herein are the property of the trademark holder. We use them for identification purposes only. This is not an official publication.

Motorbooks titles are also available at discount for retail, wholesale, promotional, and bulk purchase. For details, contact the Special Sales Manager by email at specialsales@quarto.com or by mail at The Quarto Group, Attn: Special Sales Manager, 100 Cummings Center, Suite 265-D, Beverly, MA 01915, USA.

Library of Congress Cataloging-in-Publication Data

Miguel, Jose de.
  How to build a bobber on a budget / By Jose de Miguel.
     p. cm.
  Includes index.
  ISBN-13: 978-0-7603-2785-2 (softbound)
  ISBN-10: 0-7603-2785-8 (softbound)
  1. Motorcycles—Design and construction—Amateurs' manuals. I. Title.
TL444.I54 2008
629.28'775--dc22

2007043915

Front cover: Jose rides one of his custom creations. *Photo by Michael Lichter.* **Inset:** A brand-new Harley-Davidson 1200-cc piston.

Title page: A line-up of Jose's custom bobbers.

Back cover: Canito's 1973 XL bobber before its custom paint job.

About the author
Former professional race car driver Jose de Miguel began building custom motorcycles in his hometown of San Juan, Puerto Rico, from necessity. In San Juan, a rider had to build his own custom bike because there were no custom shops at the time. Today he runs the thriving Caribbean Custom Cycles shop in San Juan, but he still relies on the resourcefulness and creativity that made his early builds possible.

Editor: Peter Schletty
Designer: Kou Lor

Printed in the USA

CONTENTS

	ACKNOWLEDGMENTS	6
	INTRODUCTION	7
CHAPTER 1	**BEFORE YOU START**	10
CHAPTER 2	**GETTING STARTED**	23
CHAPTER 3	**SHEET METAL**	51
CHAPTER 4	**ENGINE AND TRANSMISSION**	62
CHAPTER 5	**PRE-ASSEMBLY MOCKUP**	78
CHAPTER 6	**DISASSEMBLY**	100
CHAPTER 7	**PAINT**	122
CHAPTER 8	**FINAL ASSEMBLY**	134
CHAPTER 9	**READY TO START**	152
	APPENDIX	157
	INDEX	158

ACKNOWLEDGMENTS

This book is another step on a very long road. Nothing can be accomplished without the help and support of others. No man is an island, or so the saying goes. So this is my chance to thank all those who have been there since the beginning, throughout, and still will be there when this motorcycle trip is over.

First and foremost, I need to thank my parents, Carmiña and Guti, who have always (sometimes reluctantly) backed me and my crazy ideas, decisions, and total sense of adventure. Thank you to my "abuelo" (grandfather) who paved the path towards that sense of adventure and uniqueness.

Thank you to all those who motivate and inspire me, from all walks of life, alive or dead:

To my friends here in Puerto Rico who ride my bikes, who are always there when needed to surf, party, or take time from their lives to help me out.

To the ones involved in the industry, many of whom are my true peers that I've known for a very long time. We share events, tips, parts, work, housing, a space on the trailer, and way too many things to write here. Hank, Jesse, Sugar Bear, Johnny, I.L., the list goes on.

To my friends in Hawaii, who have shown me a second home throughout the years.

To my friends in Latin America who follow what's going on, and who I have been proud to represent in this custom bike world. Vale!

To my friends all over the world, from Japan to Finland, from the U.S. to Singapore, those who have shown me support along the years, bought my shirts, read my crazy shit, and have been following this crazy ass trip.

To those who some call fans but I simply call friends, thanks for shaking my hand and thanks for the good words.

To Darwin, JoAnn, and Peter, thanks for the help and the ride.

To Michael Lichter, *Motorcycler*, and everyone else for taking such cool photos.

To everyone that has passed by and influenced me on this rollercoaster ride we call life, good or bad, friend or foe. The good makes the path smoother, happier, and easier. The bad makes you stronger, helps you learn and work harder.

To all those who took the time to write a book so I could enjoy reading it.

To those who composed music, so I could enjoy listening to it.

To all those who have been able to "grow" and make something of themselves, no matter the odds.

To my home, Puerto Rico, from San Juan to Rincon, I am indeed a very lucky person to have been born here.

Gracias a todos…siempre.

INTRODUCTION

These pages reflect over 15 years experience building bikes. We have lived through many eras and many fads, and I believe if this book had been published three years ago, many of you would not recognize the bikes or would simply refer to them as things of the past. Many of the bikes you will see featured here—what I call my bob/chops—are heavily based in the past. When catalogs were few, parts hard to get, and "custom" meant building it by hand, money was not the main motive for the build. Many, many guys went before us, lit the torch, and worked until the late hours in their garage, tool shed, or shack to create what they believed to be the ultimate piece of coolness: their own bobber or their own chopper.

I am as intrigued by the past as I am by the present, by bikes that have endured time, bikes that are still cool, even if they are 30 or 40 years old. With the opportunity to share with you what I do via this book, I will try to share knowledge that has been passed on to me, or stuff that I've had to wing out on my own. I'll tell you the tips and tricks I have learned along the way, just trying to make life a bit easier. I will also share brilliant examples of other builders' work to demonstrate what this lifestyle and art (and this book) are all about.

This book is about building an inexpensive chopper or bobber. Notice that I don't use the word cheap. It's not about being stingy. It's about being able to recognize what is needed to be able to create something, not exactly because we are saving money, but because it's a lot more satisfying to be able to create something on your own, something with your hands, and to realize the endless possibilities of your imagination. It's about being able to look around and recognize stuff, parts, or whatever it is that can be of purpose toward your final goal of building a cool bike.

In most of my builds, catalogs and high-end billet parts are avoided. We try to work with what we have, but when we do use something from a catalog, the reasoning is simple: new is new. For electronics, tires, and other such items, you are always better off with brand-spanking-new, out-of-the-box stuff. I should also add that although you might see a couple billet items on some of these bikes, it's not blasphemy. It's just that they were lying around and were used as needed.

The first rule of this book is that there are no rules. I don't mean that you should go to your local hardware store, tractor supply, auto store, antique store, etc., and buy everything you see, or rip off parts of your wife's kitchen to accomplish your build. No, that won't cut it. But if you see something that catches your eye, and you feel it will fit your bike smoothly, then go ahead and try to make it work. Remember, the key word is smoothly. I personally dislike stuff that sticks out like a sore thumb and is just there because someone wanted to put it there.

Here comes the second big word to live by: purpose. Everything should have a purpose. The bikes you will see here (and we joke about it constantly) won't run if something falls off. Everything is needed, and everything is more or less vital.

Of course, this will all be a challenge—a challenge to yourself and a test of abilities. And just because the book says something doesn't mean it's written in stone. We all have different levels of ability, and to be able to complete any of these projects you need a certain amount of how-to, welding, fabricating, cutting, and mechanical knowledge. It would be difficult to list all the skills involved, but the beauty of these bikes is that there's always someone who enjoys working with them just as much as you do. And who knows, he might

This is a pretty good example of a Frisco-style bike.

Another perfect example of a Frisco-style, straight from Frisco.

The Hawaiian Local Boy style.

This is a very good example of a Puerto Rican "Tuca"-style.

have some talents that he is willing to pass on to you. I guess, in short, it's always good to have friends, mentors, and even other reference books to go to. I am self-taught in everything I use today, from the welder to the lathe. I can tell you, that is the hard and long way to do it, but sometimes you are better off. Even professional builders don't know it all, but knowing enough of as much as possible is a good start. There's no shame in calling a friend (yes, I still do) and asking him a couple questions about any certain chore.

Again, the purpose of the book is not being cheap, much less stubborn. If there's something you can't handle, let someone else do it. Riding around on your very first welds is not very safe. Make sure the guy who's doing the job is cool enough to give you pointers, or maybe a lesson. Every day that you learn something new is a worthwhile day.

I work on bikes day in and day out. I have built many bikes, and I've seen many fads fade away. I've dealt with the wide tire/super-big motor craze, and I'm still around doing what I enjoy the most. Another key word: enjoy. Sure, we build bikes to impress others (to impress girls, mostly) or because we believe they are the epitome of cool. But the real main purpose is having something that you built, and you are riding and enjoying.

As a professional bike builder (if you want to call it that), I obviously have as many tools as possible, tools for each and every job, and the knowledge of how to use them. That is a very large investment in order to build your own inexpensive bob/chop. We all know life is easier with the right tools, but don't go running to the store to fill the tool box, buying the hottest welder and plasma cutter, or you will end up with the most expensive inexpensive bike ever. Don't go crazy and try to do everything by yourself, either. Again, there's no shame in having someone do something for your bike (most of us do it). What's the sense of making your own tank if it takes you three years and you have to buy thousands of dollars worth of equipment? Well, that's what this book is about—look around, find that old beat-up tank, and get to work. Use your brain. Move to the next problem, cut the tank, fabricate this and that . . . etc.

Pride is fine, but when you work within a time frame, pride is money. I have friends who finish my gas tanks for me. Sure, I cut them up, shape them, and tack them, but then I put them in a box, send them to another shop, and let them deal with the rest. As a business owner, I am dealing with time. And by the time I am done with the tank, the electric bill, welding supplies, gas, and more time, the tank is one big expense. (And this book is all about keeping expenses down.) If I had all the time in the world, and not 11 bikes waiting to be built, then I might invest the time and money. But if those guys are experts at what they do, and the turnaround is super quick, I give them the job every single time.

I guess what I am trying to say is that there's a thin line between doing it yourself and spending way too much money and time (worse yet, a crappy tank in the trash can). And that's the way it is with every single part of the bike build.

CHAPTER 1
BEFORE YOU START

MY HISTORY OF CHOPPERS AND BOBBERS

Most of us know the history of where bobbers or choppers came from, the textbook history of how stock bikes became customs and got their proper names. But I'm interested in the modern rebirth of customs. Not the high-dollar super custom chops that we see at rallies or on TV, but the simple, soulful bikes built as everyday rides.

To me, the turning point in all this new bobber rage started a couple years ago with an exhibition at the Journey Museum in South Dakota. There's a new guard in the industry today: guys like Indian Larry, with all his amazing creations; Billy Lane with the *Devil in a Red Dress*, the blue Shovel chopper, and the *Knuckle Sandwich*; Chica; Hank Young; Johnny "Chop" Vasko; and several others. They've all made

Wicho's 1952 Panhead
Wicho is an old friend. I have worked on all of his bikes over the couple of decades we have known each other. We found this bike in Miami. It belonged to another friend of ours, a tattoo artist. It was bought, ridden to Daytona, and shipped to Puerto Rico.

The bike was put together by Warren Lane (Billy's brother), and when we got it to the shop, it went through a transformation of sorts. Although we did not change anything major from Warren's original plan, the wheels received a coating of spray-can red, and the whole bike got a bunch of spray-can flat black. The seat was reupholstered in Zodiac fabric, and the bike got new bars, a jockey shift, new bearings, an open primary, whitewall tires, etc. The bike was riding well, so the motor and transmission were untouched (until a few years later, when they were rebuilt). This particular bike was one of my first and is still one of the crowd's favorites. I built it way before bobbers became mainstream.

Curt's 1979 Shovelhead
Curt was one of our local military customers. One of his friends was shipping out, and he bought this 1979 Shovel from him. It's slightly based on Wicho's 1952 Panhead. Again, we kept as much as possible from Curt's donor bike, using one of our rigid frames with fat bob mounts. Since Roosevelt Roads closed, all my friends from there were transferred to other bases. This bike was delivered to Sturgis, where it got a beating (two-up).

Canito's 1973 XL
This bike has a kind of flat track look. We found this one in a garage, where it had been sitting for 16 years untouched. The frame got a rigid section, the motor was rebuilt, and the bike got new spokes, bearings, tires, and more. The oil tank is hand fabricated with an 18-wheeler exhaust pipe. The battery box/regulator/fender piece is a good example of something that can be multitasked while using minimal space. The front end is the bike's stock one, painted and shaved (legs). Everything, as you can see here, is very simple—just free-flowing lines. There are very few brand-new parts here. We used as much from the original bike as possible, while saving as much money as possible.

their style by resurrecting the simple form and style of choppers and bobbers, by being creative, and by relying on imagination and hard work. The quick growth of magazines like *The Horse: Backstreet Choppers* also influenced the rebirth of cool, inexpensive bikes on the scene.

After the Journey Museum exhibition Bob's Back by Michael Lichter, there was no doubt that simple bob/chops were here to stay. Many of the major well-known builders created bikes just for the museum, and that, to me, was the point were the ball started rolling big time. Like an omen, bobs were back and hit the industry like a swift kick to the ribcage.

If you have the fortune of being able to travel all over as I do, you will notice that certain places have certain build styles. Again, simple, inexpensive bikes, full of local flavor come by hard work, not credit cards and catalogs. Puerto Rico has the "Tucas," Hawaii the "Local Boys," Northern California the "Frisco" style, etc. They're all bikes that serve a purpose yet show the inventiveness of local home builders in creating something that was theirs and paying respect to their local environment.

I also believe that our response, in modern times, to all the overdone, bling-bling stuff that's been built since the turn of the millennium is the bobber—the simple, effective, inexpensive, but very cool bob/chop. Once more, time turned, and we became the anti-establishment builders. Many of us are not the kind to follow trends—we create them. To me, a big part of being a builder is being able to do something that is not the norm. Why? The same reason the original guys who dared to chop and bob their bikes were looking for something different and nonconforming: They wanted to express themselves and to ride what they wanted to ride, the same way it is today. Why follow? Why copy? Why?

Sure as hell, this is not total innovation. As in music, most of it has been done before. But musicians still keep on creating, using their influences to do new stuff. Modern bob/chops are influenced by everything, old and modern, new technology as well as Jurassic, used parts, new parts, and old schools of thought swirled with the newest. In short, it is a true explosion of everything and anything.

Joseph's 1971 XL
This bike was found at our local shipping company. The previous owner had bought it in the United States and had it parked at the docks for almost six years. Needless to say, seawater, rain, and dirt had taken their toll. After everything was checked, we got a Paughco rigid frame and reused the stock front end—cleaned, painted, and shaved. The gas tank is a stock Sportster tank with some changes to it and the mounts. New wheels, tires, bearings, and such completed the roller. Handmade foot and brake controls were added, too. This bike is used a lot and ridden hard. Photos were taken at Sturgis.

WHAT IS A BOBBER? WHAT IS A CHOPPER?

This will be the most confusing subject for sure. Right off the bat, I am letting you know that it is impossible to describe what defines a bobber or a chopper in detail or with accuracy. It's kind of the egg/chicken thing, and who came first? Nonetheless, I will give it a fair try. This is my opinion, and of course all opinions will vary, but this is what my eyes see and my brain computes when I see bikes.

There are styles that we recognize directly as choppers. Bobbers are way harder to define. With the recent degeneration of customs, choppers, bobbers, and whatever else people call their bikes these days, to many folks, anything and everything with a long front end is a chopper. Bare-bones, simple bikes with short front ends are bobbers. But that definition is way too ignorant and simplistic.

To aid with this, I will use bike styles by popular builders and add photos as examples. For instance, one of Indian Larry's bikes . . . just take a close look at one. What does your brain tell you? If you are saturated by the magazine/TV media, you will quickly say bobber. But to me, those are choppers. Well, let me backtrack . . . .

What I see as choppers are those cool bikes that guys started working on and building in the 1970s: the super stretched frames, front ends, king and queen seats (like

BEFORE YOU START

Omar's 1968 Shovelhead
One of our customers brought in this bike to bob/chop it. In the meantime, he lost steam and wanted to sell the bike. I called Omar right away, and in three minutes, the deal was done. This bike was the third or fourth after our Journey Museum bike. We placed everything in one of our rigid wishbone frames. Omar's gas tank was modified, a front fender from a 16-inch tire was cut up and used for the rear, and here you can see our recycled, newer Sportster front end, cut up, shaved, and painted. The rear 16-inch wheel got a fresh coat of paint, stainless-steel spokes, and a whitewall Avon tire. The front is a recycled Sportster hub laced with stainless-steel spokes and a 21-inch rim. As you see here, the bike is not completely finished. Our event in Rincon was near, and he wanted to ride . . . but it's damn near done. Photos by Motorcycler at Motorcycler.com

Captain America from the movie *Easy Rider*). Building during those times was extreme, to say the least. The longer the front end, the more radical the whole build . . . tons of chrome, Invader wheels, ape hangers, etc. What we consider choppers today are a degeneration of all this. What I call neo-choppers are what we see on TV or in magazines, even on any given Main Street, or in mega dealerships.

The word chopper comes from chopping off parts. So, in a sense, today's norm on long bikes means it's not a chopper since they add as much as possible. The most basic instinct is to call a long bike a chopper, but that's like calling a stock bike with a couple changed parts a custom.

Bobbers preceded the chopper. In the 1950s, the bobber was *the* custom. It was a very simple bike with very simple

Pichigui's 1973 Shovelhead
This bike will go on record as the fastest build I've ever done. I believe it only took a month or so. At the same time, I was building the Journey Museum bike. Our friend Hank Young found this 1973 for Pichigui in Atlanta, and we picked it up on our way up to Sturgis. He rode the bike as it was once we got there, but the next day some lady laughed at the colors, and by next morning it was spray-painted flat black (it had been white with pink and mauve). He rode the bike that way for a couple of months, and then we tore into it. This bike took a ton of really late nights. Everything moved to one of our rigid frames. The front end is the stock FXE but shaved (we had to change the triple trees). The oil tank is from Mooneyes, with Fabricator Kevin's bitchin' brackets. The rear fender came from a Triumph. We added the gas cap and changed the gas tank a bit. The rear brake is a front springer two-piston caliper from Performance Machine. This bike has a lot of details and time invested in it. After Pichigui got it and rode it to Rincon, he made a few changes. But in the beginning, it was a lot simpler and inexpensive. Again, this is a great example of what can be done. Photos by Motorcycler at Motorcycler.com

changes. Most of the changes were done to save weight and make the bike go faster. The norm was cutting the rear fender, ditching the front one, and making similar changes while retaining the stock gas tank, bars, etc. It was the typical (sort of street-legal) look of the racing bikes back then.

What everyone calls a bobber now is everything and anything that seems to have a short front end. I guess people miss the fact that the kind of bikes they are calling bobbers are actually choppers, but just the short version . . . or a different version.

When I built my bike for the Bob's Back museum exhibit, I got a ton of material to look at and help from friends like Irish Rich, who is very knowledgeable on motorcycle history. I decided on something that was in the vein of a bobber but more of a chopper. Hank Young's entry, on the other hand, went pre-bobber, more like a cool, board-track racer. A name is a name, and it often depends on what they named a type of bike in a certain era.

Since everyone has a different opinion, this is kind of a futile discussion. I call what I build bob/chops, since these bikes have traits of both bobbers and choppers. They are more like the short choppers of the 1970s and 1980s. They also have traits of board trackers and anything and everything that has influenced me.

Other custom styles include the diggers, those long, very low bikes that became so popular (Arlen Ness has some of the finest examples of these), or what I call the pro street (of the 1980s), which were influenced by speed, and maybe by drag bikes as well. The amazing part of all this is that certain areas have developed their own styles according to geography and needs. (Many styles developed by simple needs, such as lack of parts, roads, etc.)

To me, all this simply sums up to what you believe the bike is. If you see it as a chopper, well, it's a chopper to you. If you see it as a bobber, then it might be a bobber. They are all custom bikes. I define custom bikes as not coming from kits, nor having stock frames, and definitely not production bikes.

If your bike ends up looking like the ones you see here (the ones I build), it won't be a chopper, nor will it be a bobber. One thing is for sure: It will be your custom bike.

So to complicate things more, is every bike with a long front end a chopper? Might be, but I would rather say a long and tall front end defines a chopper. (Drag bikes have pretty long front ends compared to stock.) So is every bike that has something changed a custom? Don't think so. Just changing some bars or grips does not make it a custom. Customizing is not the same as a custom bike. I could write a whole book looking for variables, trying to explain the labels these bikes have acquired.

Again, it's just a name on a certain era. We would all be better off saying this is bobber-like or chopper-like. While I do have a concept of what these two styles contain, the specifics are way too varied to be able to pinpoint. To top it off, some of the modern bikes have traces of all the styles, from the past and present, like mutts.

Bikes and their names can be separated by eras—that is for sure—although modern bikes carry traces of every single style, with a mix and match of parts and hints of what was once recognized as a must-have to be able to call it a precise name. I even have my own names to describe certain custom bikes, and some are too harsh to be published here. Others go along the lines of bob/chop, neo-chopper, etc.

If you want to be a purist, then this whole thing gets even more complicated. Then again, why complicate our already complicated lives with such trivial questions as "What is my bike?"

To end all this, I will try to show some cool examples of what I consider a true bobber or chopper, bob/chop, pro street, etc.

Modern bikes are a total mixture of everything and anything, even those we call bobbers or choppers. They have parts, colors, and fabrication that were not available back then. They have modern brakes mixed and matched with old stuff, such as engines or springers. More so, the wide-tire craze ends up being closer to pro street–style bikes than actual choppers, although tall choppers with wide tires are a mix of both . . . .

So the story goes on and on. And I have limited space here. So let's get on with building a bike.

WHAT TO LOOK FOR

I can only talk about what I know and normally use, and that's older Harley-Davidson (H-D) motorcycles. But this book can apply to what you are building and can be taken as a basis for any build. I have seen many cool bikes done with different engines, brands, and styles in the past few years. Be it Harley, Triumph, or any Japanese bike (Honda, Yamaha, etc.), even European makes, any bike can become the heart of your build. These instructions can be used for anything and everything.

Since I am partial to old Harleys, to me the perfect start would be a Panhead, those motors Harley used from 1948 until 1965. Although I also dig Knuckleheads (1932–1947) and Shovelheads (1966–1984), anything will do.

You should look for complete bikes, preferably running. The reason you should favor a running bike is very simple: If the bike already runs, the amount of surprises (and expenses) will be lowered substantially. Compare the price of a running bike versus a basket case.

A view of a Panhead engine. These lasted from 1948 to 1965.

BASKET CASES
Basket cases are bikes in pieces. They're always advertised as complete but seldom are.

Since this will be a budget build, look around, be savvy with your hard-earned money, and don't be stubborn. Let's say you are dying to have a 1965 Panhead (who isn't?), but you're having a hard time finding one. You find a fair-priced Sportster. Think about it. I would go for the Sportster because having a bike you're not 100 percent happy with is better than none at all. And you can always sell it if the elusive Pan happens to show up.

This was a normal custom hop-up in the 1970s. Builders would start with a Panhead engine and modify it to use Shovel heads and cylinders.

Sportster engine.

At our shop, we have built several Sportsters and are in the process of building a few more. In this case, Sportsters happen not to be popular bikes, so they can be found cheap and make a great end product (read: your cool bike).

I have seen a lot of cool Brit bikes, so keep an eye out for them. They're another source that can be found for a very fair price. Look around on websites, shows, magazines, and such for very good examples of finished bikes. (At the end of the book, I will give links to several friends who happen to work with the various brands I am talking about.)

Japanese bikes can be found for almost nothing and are a very good resource for your project, although I believe they take a lot more work since catalogs are mostly filled with H-D compatible parts.

So once you start looking, what should you look for? Well, as I said before, try to make up your mind, but keep an

Two views of a cone Shovel motor, circa 1970 to 1984 (kidney-style Shovels were available from 1966 to 1969).

This is a totally redone 1965 Panhead motor, the one I used on my Journey Museum bike.

open mind as well. Look around, ask your friends, check the Internet, read the classifieds, and use any and all sources that you might come up with.

I would strongly suggest that you look for a complete bike, running if possible, and I will explain why. A complete bike will have parts that you will use, trade, swap, or sell for other parts you need. A running bike will have everything you might need; it will limit the surprises and the extensive parts search and make it easier on your pocket. Also, it could be ridden as an ongoing project, meaning you will enjoy the bike while setting everything up for the build. You should balance the (probably) higher price of the bike against what it will actually cost to fix those dreaded unforeseens. Remember that the trick here is a low-buck bike.

I do not pay much attention to the overall condition of the bike in my builds. Most of it is coming apart and will be redone our way, so that is of no major concern. As long as the bike is strong, the motor and transmission are running,

A 4-speed "ratchet"-top Harley transmission.

A 4-speed "cow flop"-style transmission.

we are already ahead. If you wanted a springer front end badly and the bike you are considering buying already has it, well, more power to you. But if it does not, it shouldn't affect your decision. You can add one later. If the frame is bent or cracked, but you are planning on changing the frame anyway, well, it's of no concern either. What is important to me is that the parts I plan on using are in good condition.

I always use the engine and transmission. Sometimes, I use the wheels, front end, clutch, rear drum brake, gas tank, and more. With Sportsters, we use the frame and add a weld-on rigid section. Those are the components you will need to take a closer look at. Decide if you want the oil tank or anything else for that matter. That mental list should rule the decision you make in buying the perfect bike to start your build.

Let's not forget the most important of all: the paperwork. Clean, legal papers will make your life a hundredfold easier when it comes time to register the bike, sell it, or get pulled over by the cops.

The better overall condition your new bike is in, the better odds of selling what you won't use and hence starting the build fund. It's true, however, that even a running bike may be a death trap. Look at the cases, the transmission case, heads, cylinders, etc. I go by what is irreplaceable, or the most expensive to replace, and I make my way down. Prepare a checklist if you must; do it by importance. For me, it's second nature, but I recommend writing it all down, and ask as many questions as you feel like. If you do not have much experience, bring a friend with you, or ask as much as you can before purchasing or deciding.

An Evolution 5-speed transmission.

> If I had to make a list of what I've seen as inexpensive bikes for projects, it would be something like this (from cheapest to most expensive):
>
> 1. Japanese
> 2. Harley Sportsters, British bikes (Triumphs, Nortons, etc.)
> 3. Big Twin Harleys, Evos, Shovels, Panheads, Knuckleheads (in that order)
>
> Again, this is not the Gospel According to Jose, but it's the norm.

I've tried to write a list of what to look for when buying a used bike. The only problem with doing so is that I do not know what you want, what you will use or rip off the bike, what you'll buy and hate later . . . of course, the variables are infinite. What I can certainly say is that you need to do your homework. You have to figure out what you want to do, how your build will look as an end product, what brand or type of bike appeals to you the most, and what bike has parts available and will be easier to work on. That list will be a much better guide than mine. For example, let's say you are looking at a 1972 FL Harley. In your build, you want 16-inch wheels, a wide-glide front end with nacelle, fat bob gas tanks, an enclosed primary, long fenders, etc. Well, that FL has most of what you want, so you are golden.

I know the going rate for these bikes and can find a deal without much sweat. To tell you the truth, I am not very analytical about the whole thing. I give it a quick once over and decide. Sure, there are all kind of folks. I guess part of my reasoning is that many of these bikes are just becoming scarce, rare, older, and therefore more expensive. What you consider a good find today might be an impossible one in a couple years.

To me, the most important components are the engine and transmission, since those are the heart of any and every build and something you will keep for sure. So you should pay attention to those.

Front ends are inexpensive to replace, so their condition is not important. If your donor bike has a springer and it's bent, you'll more then likely trash and replace it with new parts.

The best piece of information I can give you is simply to do the homework, have an idea of what you want—what you would like your bike to look like, what style of bike you want—and use that as your guideline when you shop around.

Good luck, and have fun. To me, this is the coolest part of the build: the hunt. And now we start visualizing the bike for the first time.

Above: *A view of the 5-speed transmission sprocket after it was installed (we use chains in all our builds).*

Right: *A 1965 4-speed transmission being rebuilt, without a kicker mechanism.*

CHAPTER 2
GETTING STARTED

PREPARE YOURSELF

We all need to begin with something, maybe an idea or a bike we have seen and badly want. Some of us have a preference for certain engines and certain years. In reality, any cool, inexpensive bike can be built with any Big Twin or Sportster. It's what you make of it that makes that end product cool and the owner/rider proud.

By experience, builders have all started on the wrong end of the build many times. Maybe a frame here, or a motor there . . . nothing wrong with that. Sometimes, deals show up and we can't let them pass, but since we are kind of following what I do at the shop, let's start by what I start with: the search.

You might be lucky enough to already own a bike that you want to use for your project. Maybe that old Shovel, or even better, a Panhead, is sitting around your uncle's garage and he never uses it. Maybe, if you are not that lucky and have to look around for your donor bike, well, that kind of gives you a better spectrum of choices.

What I do is talk to the customer and kind of figure out what his budget is (how much money he can hide away from his spouse). Of course, I try to find the most inexpensive bike possible if the customer is not set on a year or engine configuration. I start the search by calling friends, asking other shops, and even looking around while driving. (Believe it or not, I've found a lot of bikes that way, just sitting alongside the road with a "for sale" sign.)

If there's no bike to be found, or the prices are too high, then I hit the Internet or newspaper classifieds. I search areas

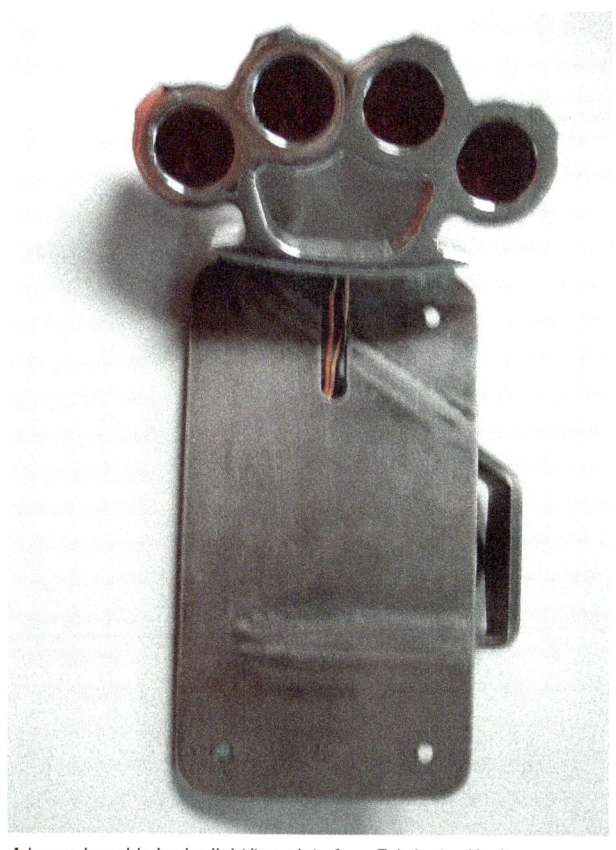

A brass-knuckle brake light/tag plate from Fabricator Kevin.

A complete OEM Harley-Davidson white rubber kit. These are really hard to find. A friend sent me these to use on the Journey Museum bike.

closer to home, or maybe an area where I know someone who can check it out and/or pick up the bike for me.

Once the monetary exchange takes place, the shipping and any other tasks, then it's time to plan your build.

I don't have the gift of being able to draw. I do it all by what is stored in my mind. I write down notes, I make lists of what I want to do, parts I need, even paint color and scheme, and I make the list as detailed as possible. I even do crude plans of what I want it to be. Let's say I'm working on foot controls. I piece them together, part by part, so I know what needs to be done. For example: two 1-foot metal rods, two bungs 1/2-inch long, two bolts, fabricate two tabs, and such. Then I go into how I will bend them, where will I weld, so on and so forth.

The whole finished bike is already on my mind before I start. Sure, I change stuff as I go along, but I end up with 90 percent of my original plan. If I knew how to transfer my

> A bung is a small, threaded piece of metal welded to the frame as an attachment point. Sometimes it's a threaded nut, and sometimes it's a specially fabricated piece. In any case, you want the threads to be deep enough and the weld strong enough for whatever it's supporting (fender, gas tank, seat, etc).

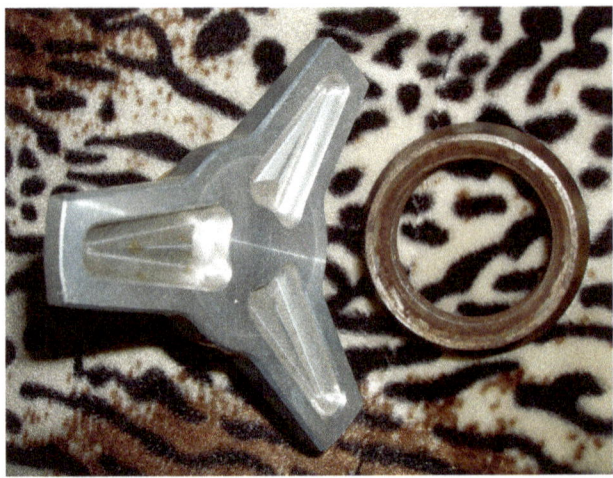

Spinner gas cap and bung.

ideas to paper, you would be able to see how close the idea is to the actual bike.

I build bikes for a living, so it might be easier for me to figure out what I want, but sometimes it's not. You see so many bikes and so many cool things that you try to avoid them in order not to copy anyone. That is the hard part of being original. Sure, some stuff is very similar and it's impossible to change; but still, creativity is really high on the list. So for you, it's great to have all those examples of cool bikes—go to the events, take photos of what you like, check out magazines, websites, anything and everything. Information is crucial and will give you a better understanding of what you want. I don't mean for you to go get a photo and copy what you see. Just use it as a base, a starting point, and then add a little or a lot of your own personality into it.

Again, when you build a lot of bikes, the challenge is to do something that people can see and recognize as your work. For example, on my bikes I believe it's the end product as a whole and not a certain thing that makes people notice and know it's from our shop. With photos as your guide, you can even go with a certain style, maybe a look, or just a stance that is a very good starting point. Compare it with what you see in similar bikes, maybe mid controls, for example, forward or floorboards. Many times you can make life easier by just using what you have. But if you definitely must have it, check out how it looks first.

Another good idea is taking ideas from others who have done it before. If you look at my bikes, the front end is from a Sportster. I started using them because I had a bunch at the shop that people had left behind. They were there, and they were free. So why not? Besides, I really dig that narrow look. So we cut off what we did not need, like tabs and bosses for the front brake and fender, passed them through the lathe, and polished or painted them. There we go—a unique front end with just a bit of work.

Some of the parts for the Chop-Off bike: brass risers from Misumi in Japan, kicker pedal from Fabricator Kevin, and custom drill-bit foot pegs.

Our custom tail light/tag plates to use with old-style brake light (available at our shop). We use these in most of our bikes.

Another gas cap. Billy Lane does this for his oil caps, but they are big enough for a gas nozzle to fit (these are vented).

A billet transmission plug. We use these for 5-speed transmissions to cover the speedometer sensor hole (since we don't need no stinking speedos).

There are lots of very inexpensive front ends out there. Another common find is a 19-inch wheel that someone has discarded for 21s or billet wheels. I use 19-inchers all the time, so take the idea and roll with it.

Maybe you saw a certain builder do something out of nothing. Go ahead and steal his idea. That might be the finishing touch you were looking for or the cure for that headache that has been bugging you for days.

Since this is the getting started chapter, start your mental list. Get your pad, and start writing it up. Look around your garage and see what you can use. Check the donor bike for stuff you can keep, for sure.

I make a separate list for items I need to order and another one for items I will have to find by alternative means. Every time I find an item, I check it off the list.

Remember, the list will grow, no matter what. You will forget or simply change your mind. I always stick to my guns throughout the majority of the project because (most of the time) the first idea is the best one.

So you happen to be looking at the bike you are about to disassemble. Take the time to check it out, compare what you have to what you want, list the parts that will be used, and take a lot of photos from the beginning to the end. Not only do they look cool in your before-and-after scrapbook, they also help in getting an idea of how parts looked before you started, how they fit together, or even the direction of the fender struts (don't laugh, I've forgotten before).

Let's say you are using a rigid frame (which is all I use). Well, that rear banana brake won't fit, so take it off the list. Sell it or swap it for something you might use. If you have a

These are old brass manifold clamps. I don't believe they make them anymore. Still, they are cool.

Magnetos are very cool. If your bike already has one, it's a big plus, because they are not cheap.

An original Harley Fat Bob gas tank.

wide glide but you want to use a narrow, do your thinking—the pros and cons—and decide.

The hardest part of all this planning is the paint. To some people, it's almost impossible to make their minds up about what they want. Of course, if you are going the super-inexpensive spray-paint way, well, skip this part. Rattle flat black for $2.89 will solve all the headaches, but some of us like to use colors. Metalflake and shiny kandies give the bike a certain appeal (more so to the female counterparts). Yeah, Harleys are meant to be black, but there are so many cool colors and combinations out there, go crazy, and have fun.

Again, check everywhere for cool paint on bikes. There are a lot of ideas out there, and you will be able to more or less see the result without having to paint your bike first. Look around for what your friends use for color schemes, and try to stay away from their colors while still finding some inspiration. No matter how cool they seem to you, you don't want to end up looking like Ponch and Jon Baker on an episode of *CHiPs*.

A stock FX/FXE Superglide-style gas tank.

A Mustang-style gas tank.

ECONOMICS AND THE MONEY DILEMMA

The hardest part of building a bike is money—saving money, finding inexpensive parts, and using as much as you can. As we all know, money is the root of all evil. But we need it.

So how much will this whole project cost you? How much will you have to beg, hide, and trade? Well, I guess it depends on your budget.

We are not building a $50,000 bike here, that's obvious (hint: read the title). Then again, it's not a $100 bike either.

I would say that bikes similar to the ones seen here will set you back anywhere from $4,000 to $28,000. As you already know, options are so vast that it's difficult for me to put a price on what you have in mind or to know what kind of budget you're comfortable with.

So the budget is up to you. My bikes end up being anywhere from $10,000 to $18,000 (labor and parts, including donor bike). For a custom bike built with a classic original motor, paint job, labor, etc., that's not much. Of course, this all depends on what you have. If you already have that Sportster, Triumph, or Shovelhead engine on-hand, well, that's a big chunk of the budget that you already have covered.

For this equation to be successful, the price range on the donor bike should be from $1,000 (or less) to $9,000 (with a lot of working components you'll keep).

Since you have an interest in doing it yourself (since you are reading this book), that should turn into big savings. Even though you won't be paying big labor costs to pro shops, there will be some chores that should be done by professionals and should be calculated into your budget. We'll get into these in future chapters.

I've seen people work on bikes themselves but end up at some shop since they can't get it running in the end. Price-wise,

Two examples of a peanut-style gas tank.

GETTING STARTED

A prism-style gas tank.

it will hike up your project since any shop worth its salt will check everything on your bike before letting you hit the road, no matter if the bike is just there to have its electrics checked.

There will be some parts you'll get from a catalog. I mentioned tires, bearings, and such, but people also tend to get carried away with the shiny stuff. Let's take a headlight as an example. On my bikes, I use what I call the cheapo lights, ranging from $30 to $50 in catalogs. They are simple enough, work fine, and look good enough to use. Then again, a fresh coat of paint can do wonders to a headlight and improve the flow of the project.

As we tend to follow a pattern in our shop (using similar items/parts for our bikes), we end up using similar (if not the exact same) gas tanks for our builds. These tanks go from $75 used to $100 new. Since we will cut them up and mold them for the bike, the latest and newest gas tank makes no difference to us.

If you are catching my drift, and I've said it before, imagination takes you a long way and saves you money. So here I am, just giving average prices for some items and leaving you to figure out the rest. For example, a good paint job, which will last the life of your bike, starts around a grand. And it's well worth it. Good materials to do that same job yourself will be around $500. But remember that your bike is only as good as the paint; that is what attracts the eye. And a shitty paint job will turn into a much larger expense later on when you have to take the whole bike apart and reassemble it for a new paint job. In my shop, we use a lot of paint instead of chrome. Back in the day, chrome was good, cheap, and it lasted. Thanks to EPA rules and regulations, price hikes, half-assed jobs, and peeling shiny chrome coatings, a kick-ass paint job is an even better bang for the buck.

Everything in this book is interconnected. You will find tips and ways to save or spend your hard-earned dollar throughout other chapters, and I will try to lead you in the right direction. Our customers are by no means rich people, and I prefer it like that. They are just normal everyday working guys who simply want a bike and are not afraid to help me out while working on the project.

I tell my customers about approximate final cost of the build, but I also try as hard as possible to budget it to what they can spend. You should do the same for yourself. Along with all those lists of what you need or what you want, have a budget. Check prices, once again remembering that cheap does not equal quality. I can't give all the prices on every part,

A flip-top gas cap from a boat. Gas caps can come from all kinds of unique sources.

A Zodiac-covered tuck-and-roll style seat.

but if you do your homework and figure out the normal cost of things, you will have a foundation for moving forward. If you find super cheap stuff way below the normal price range, be wary. And do not get blinded by the expensive bling-bling stuff—look at the part's utilitarian purpose and not the makeup factor.

In some cases, such as installing a rigid section (the back end of a rigid frame, readily available at catalogs), some knowledge and welding will save you a ton of money. It's way easier to add a rigid section to a Sportster frame, and the difference in cost is substantial. A rigid frame is around a thousand bucks, while the rigid section is around $200. In the case of Big Twin frames, it's about the same price range but much harder to install. Besides, you might not want to chop off that OEM frame when you can get some good money for it, maybe even enough to pay off the new rigid frame.

OEM: Original Equipment Manufacturer. This means the part is an original stock piece installed on the bike when it rolled off the factory floor or at the dealership.

We all know that parts for Harley bikes are not on the cheap side. But then again, you can get stuff at a fair price. We have all been there, thinking if one part is good, then this one that's more expensive or has the right brand name will be much better. Well, I've got a surprise for you: It's not always the case.

Let's say you can get a good pair of pistons for $60 that will work fine, or you can get a pair of high-performance pistons for $200. Sure, the well-known brand might be better, but are you building a high-performance motor? We are simply rebuilding a motor so it will work, perform, and last. Catch my drift? I'd rather have a motor that would take me from New York to Los Angeles at 65 miles per hour than a 125-mile-per-hour bar hopper.

By no means should you be cheap. And I am not suggesting you should be cutting corners. Just be smart with your money. You have no idea how many times I have heard, "Well, since the motor is apart, let's do this, and this, and this." Well, $60 for pistons, $35 for rings and such, is not a big spend. But if you have your heart set on those stroker flywheels, I guess it's time to change plans. In total contrast to what the ads, magazines, and ignorant friends tell you, if

Our flip-style sprung seat in white (from the Journey Museum bike).

you see in this book. But the techniques used here can be applied to any motorcycle brand or engine.)

The "Company" was offering some very fair-priced Evo engines and transmissions, and those are the most reliable, bulletproof motors Harley has ever built. So if you want to start your build with a new motor, it seems to be a good way to start.

Staying along the lines when you have a donor bike, it's much easier to figure out what the project will more or less cost you at the end. By experience, and counting on the parts that will be reused, I can sort of figure out how much the customer's build will cost. When a customer asks for an estimate, I'll tell them from $8,000 to $12,000, plus the price of the donor bike. That's counting labor, paint, and a high estimate (and to tell you the truth, it's a cheap estimate since labor alone would be around that much). Let's say you take $2,500 off for some of the labor you will do, still figure around $1,000 for paint (good paint). So I guess with a little adding and subtracting, you can figure out your total build cost.

I wish I could, but it's impossible to figure out what everything will cost. Also, with so many parts out on the market today, even giving ballpark figures or listing some of them will be an arduous and long list. I could list the parts I use on my bikes, and their prices, as an example. But then again, variables are plenty, and you are building your own bike, not mine. And you're doing it with parts you like and prefer. More so, what I use varies with budget and availability, and with creativity, so there's no actual list etched in stone.

your shit is working fine, keep it. There's no need for those mega motors when your 74- or 80-ci motor is working just fine and taking you (with no problems) from point A to point B.

Speaking of which, a big reason I suggest donor bikes is because a new crate motor goes for $5,000 and up, basically the same you'd pay for a complete donor bike. And as I've mentioned before, on the donor bike, you'll find a ton of other usable parts so the money will be well and wisely spent. Although, this all depends on your plans for the bike you are building. (Since my work focuses on Big Twins, that's what

The flip-style sprung seat in silver Zodiac fabric (metalflake).

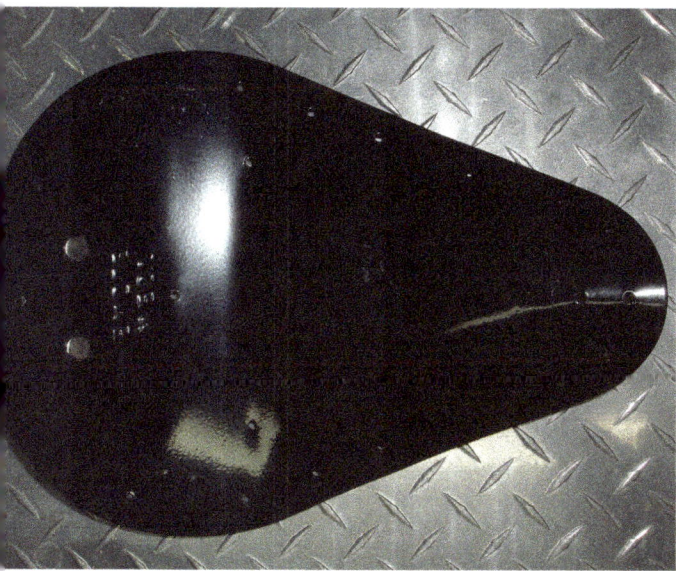

This is the seat pan that starts everything (available at our shop).

This is the seat I made for the Chop-Off bike. I bought the leather and copper rivets, had a friend sew the cover, and glued it. Total cost of materials (not including the seat pan): $15 and a few hours of labor.

GETTING STARTED

This is the same seat pan covered by our friend Paul Cox for Pichigui's 1973 Shovel.

31

Here are a couple of examples of custom-made pipes. Most of our bikes sport pipes that are made for them.

A side-by-side mockup of the actual pipes for the Chop-Off bike.

Finished product on Pichigui's 1973 Shovelhead. These have been ceramic coated.

Finished pipes on Joseph's 1972 Sportster.

Mockup of the pipes on Yuka's 1984—a new turn to the old dual FL pipes.

TOOLS

I use the tools I have. I guess what I mean is that I have learned how to use what's available to my best advantage. You get to know your tools and their tricks so well that when you end up at friends' shops you get lost dealing with the different setups on their welders, mills, or lathes.

Tools are tools, more or less. Of course, the more you have the better. The best tip I can give you is to have the right tool for the right job. You have no idea how simple life becomes when you have the toolbox to complete a job. Lucky for me, our bikes are simple so our needs are simple, as well.

Don't go out and franticly buy the whole hardware store. Sure, I do encourage you to learn as much as possible, even if that involves purchasing a welder. But if your budget doesn't allow for big tool purchases, it's a simple and inexpensive solution to have someone weld what you need. Go to the nearest machine shop so they can fabricate what you need for a little money. It's still more efficient and quick to know how to weld, plus it's another trade that you will have under your belt. So if it's realistic for you to do so, I do encourage it.

If you have any doubts about your mechanical ability, don't play macho. Ask someone who knows what they're doing to help you or show you how it's done. By no means should you stay away from the task, but help is always good. Tips and advice are treasures, and listening to someone who has done it many times before is golden. Don't be afraid to ask.

This all takes time, lots of patience, and a learning curve. Your second or third bob/chop will have a lot more of your own involvement into it, and it will become easier as you get familiar with all that needs to be done. Over time, this is what we should all aim for—having more and more of our own work and imagination put into each bike we build.

Since this book is aimed at everyone, from beginners to master engineers, we should start with the toolbox. Of course, all of us being freaks for tools (you know, typical guys), we probably already have all the basics. But I believe the juice of a good builder's garage is those special tricky tools that we actually need to make life, and the build, much easier.

Tool cabinets.

Basic Tools

- Open-end wrenches, SAE sizes (or American, forget about metrics unless you anticipate using a metric cruiser as your donor bike).
- 10-millimeter open-end wrench. Battery screws are mostly this size.
- Deep and shallow sockets. Again, SAE, but I would also have a 10-millimeter on hand.
- Socket extensions. They never hurt, ever!
- Ratchet handles. I really like to have a variety: shorter, longer, and those that flex. The more the merrier.
- Phillips and flat screwdrivers. Again, different sizes will be used. (Always remember they are for screwing, not prying.)
- Allen wrenches, sockets, T-wrenches, ball ends, short, long. As with everything else, the more the merrier.
- Torx wrenches, even though your finished bike won't have any Torx screws (we hope). Harley-Davidson loves to use them all over, so be ready.
- Hammers, an assortment: rubber, wood, all kinds. And please, don't use them to beat in axles.
- Pliers, cutters, wiring tool, strippers, snap ring tools, etc.
- Drill and drill bits. I have several drills: air, bench, electric. I can't give a specific size or horsepower for your needs, of course. But the more powerful, the better. I also have a couple that allow the chuck to open much more than standard for those big bits. And don't forget an angle drill for tight spaces; those are life savers! Makita brand has worked very well for me and takes extreme abuse.
- Hole punchers. I have them in all sizes, though I found the ones that have a spring release and mark the material when you press them are so bitchin'!
- Grinder. I have a variety of grinders for a very simple reason: I can multitask with different cutting or grinding wheels without having to exchange tools. Again, I have a couple from Makita that take a beating. The others are from various brands and seem to be taking the abuse in stride as well.

Intermediate Tools

- Grinders (electric). Having a few is much better and time effective.
- Air compressor. The air compressor size depends largely on your budget and workload. Of course, don't use that tiny one you use for filling basketballs and bike tires. It should be of enough size to be able to move that impact wrench to the max.
- Impact wrench. This is a very useful tool. I have a couple of them in various sizes. Trust me, you will use it . . . a lot!
- Assortment of air tools. When I say assortment, I mean you can never have too many tools . . . drills, grinders in different sizes, air guns, cutters, etc. You will find a use, for sure.
- Torque wrench. If you are anal about it, your bike's manual will give you the specific pounds of torque for the task at

Air compressor.

hand. It's always a good idea to follow those when working on the motor. There are different torque wrenches on the market, strengths, sizes, etc.

- Tube cutter. There are many of these available, from your normal pipe cutters to mega-buck machines. You should get the best-quality handheld one, since you want one that will move around and fit in tight spots.
- Vise. I have two or three vises of different sizes in the

Shop saw.

shop. Again, in the interest of multitasking, you should get a good-sized one that can be used for a variety of jobs.
- Tire mounting irons. Keep these on hand just in case. It's simpler to take the tire to a tire shop you trust for mounting. Always be careful, since not all setups are gentle on the wheels.
- Metal saw. Much better and quicker than a hacksaw or reciprocating saw, this tool is mobile, which is cool and will save time. Yes, precious time.
- Shop saw. I would dare say that this is one of my most used tools when building. I have two: a Makita and a DeWalt. They have taken such a beating that it's not even funny.

Advanced Tools
- Metal band saw. Although a normal band saw will do the trick with different blades, the metal saw has a variable speed which is what you need for metal, aluminum, and such. It's an expensive addition but one well worth it.
- Welder, MIG or TIG. MIG (metal inert gas) is a semi-automatic or automatic arc welding process in which a continuous and consumable wire electrode and a shielding gas are fed through a welding gun. In the TIG (tungsten inert gas) welding process, an essentially nonconsumable tungsten electrode is used to provide an electric arc for welding. A sheath of inert gas surrounds the electrode,

MIG welder.

the arc, and the area to be welded. This gas shielding process prevents any oxidization of the weld and allows for the production of neat, clean welds. Knowing both processes and having both setups is optimal, but you can use the MIG welder for almost everything, and it's much easier.

- Lathe and mill, or a combination of both.
- Plasma cutter. It's good to have it, but it's not a must-have.
- Oxy/acetylene torch. A must for heating, bending, and beating metal into submission.
- Tube bender. Although just about anything can be used to bend tubing, it's good to have a dedicated tool.
- Hydraulic press. If anything on the build needs extra-superhuman strength to insert or remove, this is a super tool to have.
- Hydraulic lift. A company called Handy makes the best in the industry, period. These are the same lifts that you see in every builder's shop and on TV shows. It's not a must, but it's damn good to have.

Metal band saw.

Milling machine.

Plasma cutter.

Expert Tools

Like I said above, you can never have too many tools, as long as they are needed for certain uses. There are so many special tools on the market, you can't even work on certain bikes without them. JIMS is one of the biggest suppliers of specialty tools for Harleys, and the tools can also be found in any of the major catalogs.

The following tools are special tools for very unique purposes but not must-haves for a shop . . . unless your name is Jesse James, and you are a master on these.

- English wheel. We have all seen this tool, probably on TV in one of Jesse's *Motorcycle Mania* episodes. It's used to squeeze and shape metal, applying pressure with your feet as you work. This tool is gaining popularity since more and more builders want to work on metal and learn more about it. It is easily found at any older car restoration shop.
- Planishing hammer. This tool presses the metal by hydraulics. It works along the lines of the English wheel. Again, you might have seen it on TV in any of Jesse James' shows. The result is similar to the English wheel, although the planishing hammer consists of two flat iron pieces that squeeze the metal.
- Sandbag, hammers. This combo is great. The sandbag is actually a leather pouch filled with buck shot you place under the metal to start molding by using hammers. There are different sizes and types of hammers for certain jobs. Chica has a piece of carved wood that he uses instead of the bag and a certain special hammer that he calls his magic hammer.

English wheel.

- Parts washer. This is a relatively inexpensive tool/machine. We use it a lot when working with older bikes (most of what we do). It works wonders on that clingy grime found all over older bikes.
- Sandblaster. Another savior, this sucker will remove paint, grime, and everything and anything that needs extra strength. Of course, having one big enough to cover a whole frame will cost a pretty penny. Then again, as they say, he with the most toys . . . or something like that.
- CNC (computer numerical control) machine. This is something all of us have wished we had at some time or another. You see this tool on all those shows where people create part after part with the push of a button (and a programmer). This is the high end of tools and requires a ton of steady work to justify its cost. However, it's on my wish list (along with a CNC plasma cutter, water jets, etc.).
- Mandrel bend tube machine. Since I'm listing dream tools here, a mandrel bend is what's used by the exhaust companies to achieve those smooth bends in the pipes. Unless you plan to start your own exhaust company, this is in the same category as the CNC—expensive.
- Metal polisher (wheel). I bought one about 10 years ago. To tell you the truth, it has paid for itself over and over. Sure, I've used it every day for years, and it might not be worth it for the casual builder. But it beats polishing by hand.
- Belt sander. Although there are many belt sanders out there, the really good ones are the expensive ones. Sure, the one from Craftsman will do the job, but it's not like having the

Metal polisher.

good industrial ones, for sure. You won't know how you managed without one. But again, it all depends on its use.

There are so many tools available. Every day, someone comes up with something new that will make your life easier and max out your credit card. This is a general guide. These are the tools I have or what I wish I had. Some of these tools are simple household tools. Others were purchased for some other special use and I have found them to be super handy when needed.

Everyday Tools
You might think I am joking when I say this, but the most useful tool in the shop is a simple Sharpie pen. I keep a bunch of them handy all over the shop, all the time. They fall into the category of "givens," tools so normal and everyday that I almost forgot to mention them:

- Measuring tape. Have normal workshop tapes as well as the flexible kind used by tailors. That will help you measure things like the circumference of a tank or the length of a curved piece of metal.
- Levels. Have a few different sizes.
- Cutting tools. Utility knives, blades, box cutters, razor blades, etc.; they'll be used for all kinds of everyday jobs.
- Tape. Have all kinds of rolls handy, from masking tape, electrical tape, thin, wide, etc.
- Chain tools. These include a chain breaker, tools for removing and installing your chain, etc.

Sharpie markers.

Tap and die kit.

Loctite thread locker.

- Zip ties, lots of them. These are great for bundling wires and cables, holding parts in place temporarily, and a million other things.
- Files. Keep your paperwork organized. Things pile up fast, such as bills, receipts, invoices, and the various design notes and mechanical info you'll need down the line.
- Tap and die kit. This will help you create fresh threads and bolts. It's a must-have in any garage.
- Soldering iron. For basic electrical work and welding small parts together, a simple soldering iron is all you need.
- Heat gun. Like a hair dryer on steroids, a heat gun is great for stripping paint, softening plastic, heating metal . . . a million things.
- Scissors. For obvious reasons.

FINDING AN INEXPENSIVE FRAME:

Since we are working on an inexpensive build, let's start with the frame. To us, this is one of the major components of the build and, needless to say, a very important one. We give a lot of care to our frames, but still we stick to very few variations of them. In other words, our frame of choice has only three or four styles, and that's about it. With all the different choices available today, we only have two meaningful differences between what we always use, and that's the engine, either a Big Twin setup (Knucklehead, Panhead, Shovelhead or Evolution) or Sportster.

We always use rigid frames fitted for stock rear tires (130 millimeters). Although you can fit a 140- or 150-millimeter tire, we seldom use anything over 140 millimeters. Our base frames have stock rake, stock downtube and backbone stretch, and wishbone downtubes. The slight variation is that we also use straight-legged downtube frames as well. When I say stock, it's based on any older frame that was actually manufactured for an FL or FX model. The downtubes happen to be the only visual or actual difference between these two frames, and these are used as the base for any of our bob/chop bikes.

For our choppers, we use a longer version of the same frame with a 2-inch stretch on the downtubes, and 35 degrees of rake on the neck. We also use these for taller riders or when using fat bob gas tanks, which tend to sit way lower into the frame and atop the engine. For the Sportster-based builds we use a stock rake, stock stretch, straight-legged rigid frame, or sometimes we use the stock frame and weld a rear rigid section. (This happens to be a very economical way to do it, but requires a bit more expertise and tools.)

All these frames above are very fairly priced. Custom Chrome distributes the Santee brand of frames, or you can find a Paughco frame at any of the other various big catalog distributors/wholesalers. Some even sell directly to the public.

We mostly use the Santee frames from Custom Chrome. Although they are a bit more expensive than the Paughco counterpart, they're well worth it. Remember that in the shop, time translates to money, so we just try to make our life much easier and our customers' pockets happier (and the purpose of this book is to make yours happier, as well).

Three major reasons I personally prefer Santee frames are:
1) Welds. This is the biggest one. We like our frames to be really clean and smooth, so the better the welds, the less grinding and molding you end up doing. These welds are smooth and very well done, which gives you a lot less headaches in the long run. Like I said, lots less grinding and a much better finish at the end product. This reason by itself is well worth the price hike over a Paughco.

Here, you can see the rigid section that will be used. We use the weld-on style, much better and stronger than bolt-on.

GETTING STARTED

Cutting the frame to allow the rigid section to fit, we also cut all the tabs and extras that won't be used in the build.

Some more cutting and a bit of grinding give the section a better fit.

We fit the rigid section onto the frame after measurements, and at a level spot, like a table, we proceed to tack and weld.

Here's the section welded into the frame.

A shot of the welded rigid section in place, with mockup wheel and everything else. We measured a few times, and everything ended up straight.

2) Accesories. Santee comes with axle, spacers, and axle nut, plus the motor mount is welded to the frame. Not only don't you have to search all over for a fitting axle and spend the $70 or more, you also don't have to worry about fitting and welding the motor mount base on the frame.

3) Fitting. We have worked with Santee frames and have never had problems with part fitment. It's been a breeze. No grinding to fit an engine, transmission, primaries, or forward controls. Again, time is money, and something that you know is going to fit right away and has fit before saves you a lot of headaches, grief, and money.

Let me give you a bonus tip: Custom Chrome (and others, I'm sure) sometimes ship orders for free to dealers. If your dealer is cool, he might pass on that savings to you. When you live on an island, like Hawaii or here in Puerto Rico, that is a really big savings since we don't have the luxury of ground shipping.

Both brands that I have mentioned here are in the $500 to $1,000 range, and both are good choices for your project. There are other quality frames in that price range, too. Santee is the better deal, in my opinion. But then again, it's your bike, it's your build, it's your pocket, so it's your choice.

Here you can see some examples of stuff that finds its way to my shop or somehow catches my attention. You might find something that will work in the least expected place. Like everything else, a few pieces are cool, but overdoing it is gaudy.

Hank Young gave me this air cleaner for my Linkert carb. It's a side vent from an antique Chris-Craft boat, also used for the port-starboard lights, and it's simply cool.

FINDING INEXPENSIVE PARTS

You might wonder where to look for inexpensive parts. Which places are the right ones to find that deal? Or how do I go about making that deal?

It does take some patience, some time, and knowing what you are looking for. Once again, good, solid preparation is the key to success. If you know what you want, and what you need, you can search for it. Keep in mind that things can and will change, ideas will produce better or worse results than you expected. But if you stick to your general plan, you'll be on the right track.

Local Independent Shops

These are gold mines. Not only do they carry the parts that dealerships won't, they also tend to have stuff that's been stocked for too long or is out of fashion and being sold at a deep discount. Or they often keep discarded parts from customers that can be had at a very good deal. They also have people walking in offering mix-and-match parts in trade. Even more important, your local shop owner (if he's experienced and not just hopping on the chopper trend) will have tons of very valuable advice, something that is worth ten times over what you'll save on a cheap mail-order catalog. The local shop, if it's been around for a long time, is the best tool at your disposal. Respect goes a long way, and in most shops it will help you develop a good customer/mechanic relationship over time. It is a treasure-trove of knowledge, tips, and tricks that can save you time and money. And if you are lucky, those guys will give you a hand through the whole build, or simply when things become confusing. I, for one, enjoy visiting these shops, talking to the owners, and snooping

I don't know what I would use a mobile home sign for, but I'm sure one of these days it might find its way onto one of the bikes, or maybe the shop wall, or eBay.

around. And you will never believe what can be found lying on a shelf under coats of aging dust.

Sadly, many of these shops are no longer around. Day by day they get crushed for various reasons, but these are the guys that have kept our lifestyle alive.

Harley-Davidson Dealerships

Believe it or not, this is the arch nemesis of the custom bike build. But you know what? There are thousands of yuppies changing their front ends, wheels, and many other parts every single day. And most of the time the owners don't even want the parts, so it never hurts asking if they have a parts storage area. Some parts can be had really, really cheap, and sometimes even free. You can find a lot of very useful parts here for your build—what's useless to some is gold to us. You can also scavenge for other stuff and resell it for more funds toward your build. I take the wheels and sell the rotors and pulley (since we don't use them) and the wheel ends up being free.

Many of these dealers have flea market sales, or they will have a table inside with a lot of stuff at discount prices. The trick is to know what will fit or what works for what you will be building. Again, some of these dealers are cool to deal with, and some are a total pompous pain in the ass. The trick here is that you need more knowledge of what you want than they do. Asking around won't be much help. If it's not on the computer or not specifically for that kind of bike, it does not exist in their eyes. Again, I am generalizing here. I've found dealers who know exactly what I'm looking for and are always willing to help. (Which is the way it should be . . . right?)

I might as well include the boutique bike shops in this section, but these are of lesser interest, since they mostly work with "custom" parts (read: shiny stuff from a catalog) and those are almost always useless for our projects. Then again, you never know. There might be something there that you need, and it might be trash to them.

The Internet

Hold on! Don't go crazy all over the Internet just yet (like eBay). I am talking about virtual swap meets. There are a ton of boards, forums, and similar places along cyberspace. These are good places to swap or buy inexpensive parts from people who know what they have, and also to

I use lake pipe covers from Mooneyes as brake pedals all the time.

sell what you don't need. There are also classifieds all over the net. This is a case where the better the homework, the better the result. It's also a very powerful tool for you to ask for what you need, because someone might have it. You can also use them for knowledge. Many of these forums have people there who really know their stuff (and some who think they do) and it's a pretty quick way to get your answers. Also remember that this is the Internet . . . it's not limited to your area. You will be amazed at how many good products come from Japan, Sweden, and similar far away places.

There are places like the Horse Backstreet Back Talk, HAMB, Shade Tree, Chopperweb, and many others. A quick search in your computer can lead you the right direction.

Try to avoid buying stuff over the Internet that you could buy at your local shop (like catalog parts) because it's much easier to go back to the shop in case there's a problem, than to ship it all over, hoping you get the right item back.

eBay
While I do use eBay, and I sell parts over it, I am very careful with it. A deal is not always a deal, and the parts are not always what you expect. Trust me, no one is out to do you a favor. Watch for the shipping prices. I only use eBay if I need something specific and have been looking for it, asking around, etc. I do auction stuff on eBay, and I run an eBay store. And who knows? I might have the part you are actually looking for. It's a great resource, maybe one of the greatest around. I have noticed that I can reach the whole world, places where shops are non-existent. Or if you live in the boonies, I have also learned that an item might be normal and plentiful in one place but impossible to find somewhere else.

Ask as many questions as possible, and choose stores or sellers that you have heard of or worked with before, or have excellent feedback. If you buy from good sellers, you'll have a better chance of getting what you need at a fair price and not getting scammed.

Thanks to my friends who work at the airport, this gas cap from an old tug will be a cool gas cap for one of my bobbers or choppers. Well, maybe not cool, but certainly different.

Also, it's one of the few places where you can search for exactly what you are looking for. Let's say you need a 1972 Harley fender tip . . . just search and you will find a bunch of choices, compare prices, and find out how much they're selling for at the moment.

I have many people e-mailing me about other sellers' parts, and I do encourage you to ask around. I make the time to check them out and give them my opinion if needed.

Again, like everything else, do your homework and use common sense. If it sounds way too good to be true, be extra cautious about it.

Since this is a budget bike, consider selling your extra parts or even stuff lying around the house that you do not need. It can create a fund for your bike project, or just earn some extra money. You never know.

Word of Mouth, Friends

A lot of times friends, and friends of friends, will have a ton of stuff laying around that you don't know of. Like everyone else, your friends have bikes, and you make new friends who happen to have bikes, so ask around. They might have a part here or a part there, or might know of someone who does.

I grew up trading stuff with friends, be it baseball cards, a cool pencil, or whatever. And when a buddy needed something (better if it was that cute girl in sixth grade) I'd give them what they needed, and they'd do the same for me. When I started on bikes, we did the same. My business was started by that theory. I traded parts with friends, worked on their bikes, installed parts, and sometimes lunch or their unwanted parts was good enough payment for me. I do have a shop, however, and I have to pay rent, bills, and all that, so it's very difficult giving stuff away.

It is natural that we create a group of friends who also ride and build. It's part of the social structure of this lifestyle, friends who will drink your beer and make your spouse mad, but will also help you with parts, tools, and work. Everyone knows someone who knows someone who might have that part or tool you need.

We also use this to find bikes, or whatever else. You never know when a friend might have a neighbor or uncle

Old doorknobs make perfect jockey shift knobs. These are actual antiques made of glass.

who has a bike at their garage that they have not used in 20 years, or that parts stash you so badly need.

Swap Meets/Flea Markets
This is one of the places I enjoy the most. There is so much stuff to be found here, bike-related or not. It's a shame I do not have the luxury of having these in Puerto Rico, but I look for them every chance I get when I am traveling.

There is a catch to these, however. Many times you have to know what you are looking for and have an idea of the prices they should be charging. Also, at big events (like Daytona, for example) they hike their prices up for two reasons: the high prices of renting a booth, and the number of ignorant yuppies looking for stuff.

But swap meets are not only a gold mine for parts, but also for whatever your imagination can create. Truck parts, boat parts, car parts, anything and everything that will fit and flow with your project can be found at a swap meet.

Look around your area for car or bike shows, or vehicle-specific swap meets in your areas that feature vendors and dealers. If it's a direct bike swap meet, most of those guys know their stuff very well. They can see a part and know what it is, the model year, bike, and more, so they are able to help you out. Even if there's stuff you do not need but can find at a super deal, those can be converted to cash later on . . . or traded for something you might use on a further build.

Closed Shops
I've searched for shops that have gone under, be it a few weeks ago, or many years ago. These guys sometimes have stock left and they might have the parts that you are looking for, but could not sell before closing. Some just throw them away or resell the lot. Others keep them since they do not have the heart to pile them in the garbage bin. Also, there are shops that might be moving and have a lot of parts they do not want to move around. I got a lot of OEM and new old stock parts when a local dealership moved, like Panhead and Shovelhead parts that they had no use for (or hadn't sold in a long time).

I have friends who have found the mother lode this way, guys with years' worth of parts saved in a container

Every time I cross the United States with my trailer, I fuel up at truck stops. These places are full of cool stuff for 18-wheelers that can be used for a bike. These look like future floorboards to me, and they will be.

Again, you can find these cool trucker chicks at truck shops all along the road.

GETTING STARTED

A cool, original Schwinn emblem will be great for the frame's neck.

since they closed the shop . . . gas tanks, glitter helmets, and more.

Other Sources

Believe it or not, antique shops are a good source of unique parts, like doorknobs as shift knobs, brass emblems, or whatever else you might think of. Tractor supply stores are full of parts you might use at a fraction of the normal cost, like trailer fenders or gas caps. Look around and you might find some cool parts that will compliment your project.

Auto parts stores can be found anywhere and offer a lot of unique pieces for your build. You have probably seen those cool oil filters on the side of the bike (the ones that Indian Larry made popular). They are simply automotive filters with a fabricated bracket. There are so many items all around. Even those dollar stores have zip ties, cheapo tools, and maybe a cheap plastic Buddha to use as a jockey shift knob.

There are so many places to look for cool parts. This is just a short list of places I tend to look. As you might have noticed, this is a never-ending quest for parts that you might use, trade, keep, sell for profit, parts that are cool, rare, vintage, antique, automotive, from boats, planes, or anything else. You'll also need some catalog parts, and there are so many catalogs out there, some with very cheap prices. Again, watch for those fishy super deals.

And I can't say this enough: Your local shop is a very good source to buy what you need, and you will be supporting those guys and keep the shop going. In these days of shops closing on every corner and catalogs all over the place, trust me, they need it. Support your local independent shop.

CHAPTER 3
SHEET METAL

GAS TANK

Let's go back to the pre-planning stage. If you have done your homework, you know more or less which style of gas tank are you leaning toward and what needs to be done in order to mount and fit it. Plan the way the brackets, bungs, and gas cap will be placed. Such little annoyances are common, and many tend to forget.

So what do I use? Well, I stick to certain tank styles, but the basis for the final product comes from Sportster gas tanks (the older style) and classic peanut tanks. We also use one commonly called the chopper tank, or a smaller version of the Mustang and fat bob tank. We use several different tanks and modify them to our needs, to the bike, and to the way it will look once everything flows.

Depending on your ability, time, and finances, do what you need to do. We modify every single one of our tanks, from a minimal inexpensive change that can be done simply and quickly to cutting the whole thing up and rebuilding it, just short of fabricating the whole tank.

Remember, inexpensive does not mean cheap. We pride ourselves on building clean bikes with lots of details that are oblivious unless you really take the time to look into the build (and sometimes have a certain knowledge). For example, we change the tunnels on our tanks to what we need according to the height, depth, and the way it will sit later on the backbone. We weld bottom mounts, change the fuel petcock position, play around with different gas caps, and more. It could be as simple as welding a rod down the center of the

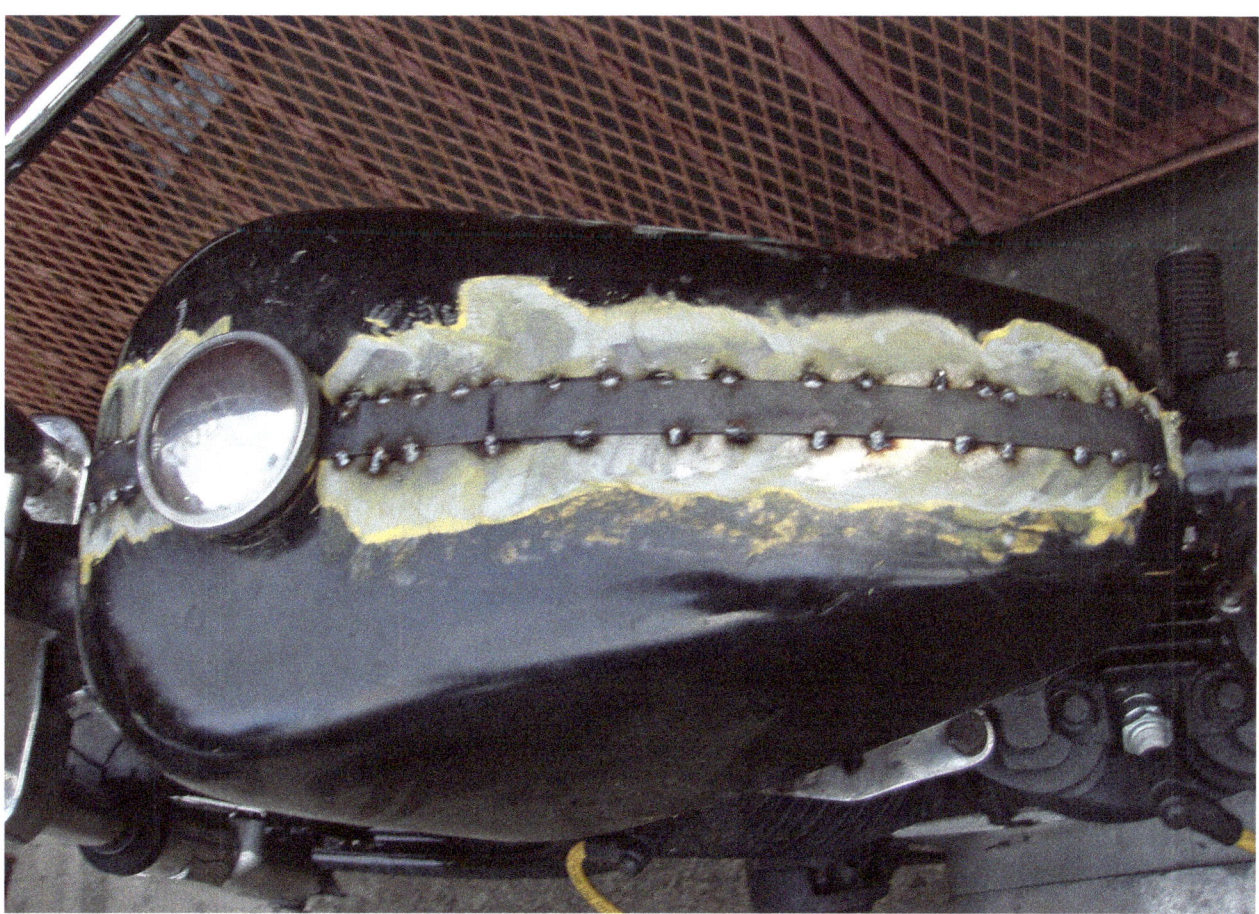

This is a stock Sportster tank. We welded a metal strap through the center to match the one in the fender. This is very simple to do and gives the tank some texture.

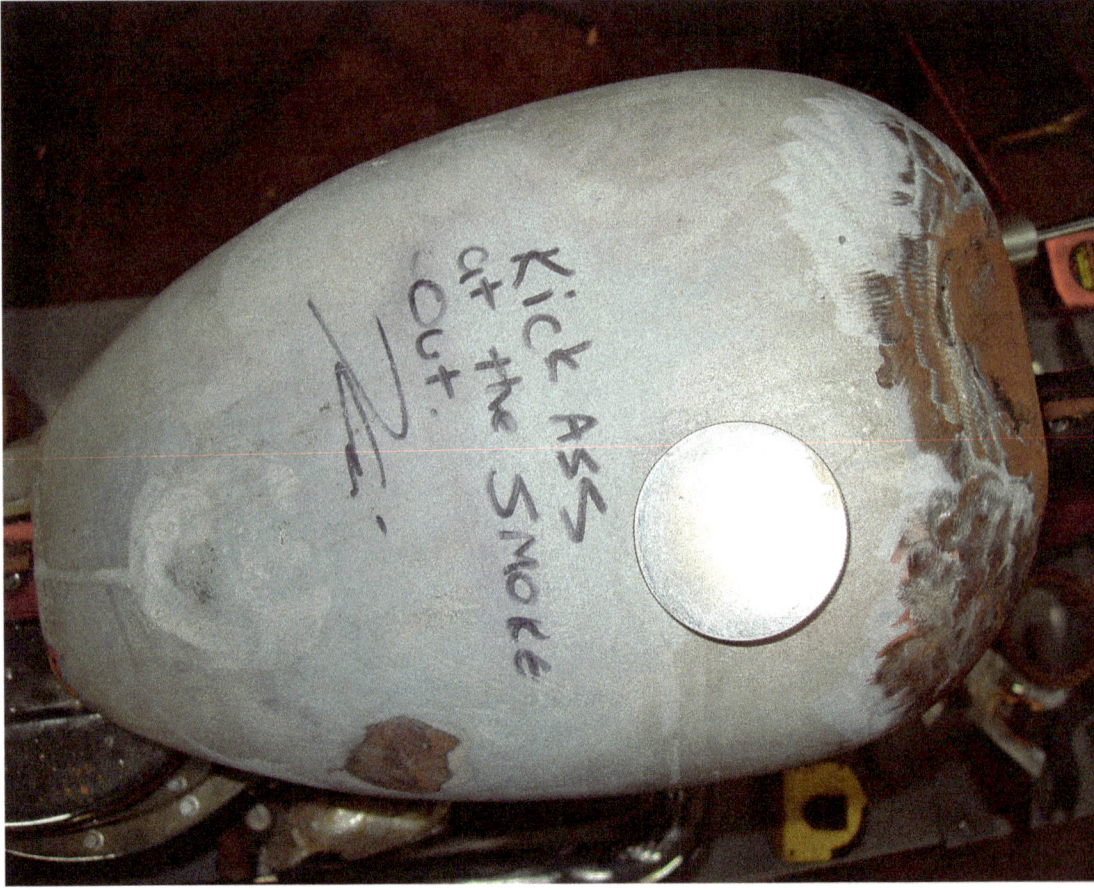

The tank on our Chop-Off bike. This is a Wassel peanut tank. It was badly beaten, but we fixed it to look like new.

gas tank or cutting it all up, reducing metal from the center and bottom and adjusting the length.

You can do wonders with inexpensive steel rods twisted to modify your tank. Just add a little imagination and lots of creativity. Metal is the coolest medium to work with; just take a look at what Indian Larry and his crew used to make gas tanks and other metal parts. Who would imagine taking the time to bend metal would end up looking so cool?

I really dislike gas tanks that look out of place. Sometimes they're either too long or they seem like they belong on someone else's bike. It's just not my cup of tea. To me, the whole placement, the way it sits on top or on the backbone, should flow and keep the same lines as the fender, oil tank, front end, bars, and such. We place the gas tank several times, mark the spots where it could go, and each and every time we stand back as far as possible to feel how it stands, looking for that line and flow until it looks just right.

Since we use the bottom mounts and other ways of holding the tank, I will try to explain our process for installation. We measure the width of the backbone, measure the width of the tunnel, and cut the mounting tabs accordingly. (We also readjust ourselves and relocate the frame's center line constantly before starting any welding or fabrication.) We always leave extra material when we make our cuts, and with patience and time we grind off material until it's a close fit (almost perfect). Remember, we are working right now with the bottom mount tabs, so appearance isn't everything.

This is our normal bottom mount. The tank was a stock Sportster tank, and the bottom was made by our friends at Twisted Choppers in South Dakota. Notice that I welded a round stock rod around the edge of the gas tank.

A top view of the same gas tank. Here we changed the gas cap to a spinner-style. Notice the covering of the old hole.

We install rubber grommets and bolt the mounts to the gas tank, and then we mount the tank once more. If it looks right, we tack weld the mounts in place strong enough to hold the weight of the tank but enough that it will not be a pain to remove them and align again later on. We align the gas tank with a mixture of levels, measuring, and eyeballing. This is a tedious procedure. It takes time and patience to place the tank and take it off several times until it's right. Once this is all done and the tank is fastened in place (with new grommets) and tight, it should not be leaning to a side or out of whack. If it's not, then your job is done, and you can weld the mounting brackets in place for the final assembly process. Remember, all this is done with the bike frame totally level.

Tip: Here's one of the most valuable tips I have ever heard, and something to live by: "Never expect an imperfect human to achieve perfection." We build stuff so it looks right (sometimes to the extent of doing and redoing it). But don't fret if it's not perfect. I've always believed a bit of guesstimation is gold.

The other two most common ways to mount gas tank tabs are with the eared-style tabs on top of the tunnel or the tabs on the side. For easier description purposes, I will call them top mount, side mount, and the already talked about bottom mount.

A regular (standard or stock, anyway you want to call it) would be a side mount. In this case, what we do is measure from tab to tab (inside). Since we are mounting this gas tank Frisco style (atop the backbone), we cut and bore a piece of round steel stock to the width measurement taken before. This bung, as it's called, will sit atop the backbone for the front mount and will hold the tank either by being bored through or by being drilled and tapped for two bolts.

The rear mount takes the same process. Instead of welding it to the top, we angle the tank according the backbone, mark it, drill through, and install. Then we weld it in place. We always use a through bolt with a nut. This way of mounting the rear is much stronger, and it has never failed us, plus it keeps the strength and integrity of the tube.

We use a similar procedure when mounting the tank on top. We fit, sit, and mark. Once we know where the tank will live, we mark and drill the holes on the backbone (this time

Notice the molding on the frame and how it matches the gas tank. It just sits flush. This is a very old-school look.

on top). We fabricate the bungs, drill and tap them to the correct bolt measurement, and then we install and weld all around, creating a very solid mount. Again, this is a very strong and secure way of mounting a tank.

Remember that a full tank of gas is very heavy, so a solid mount is a must. Vibration can do a lot of damage, and tabs can be broken off. We never realize how heavy fuel is until we have to carry that 5-gallon jerry jug.

Sometimes we use fat bobs, but those are simple, straightforward mounting jobs. And sometimes, or should I say most of the time, we can't leave anything alone, so we also get working on those, too. You can do anything to them and make them look cool while leaving them in stock configuration, or cut them up, go crazy, and make what my friend Sugar Bear calls "slim bobs."

REAR FENDER

In case you are already wondering, yes, *a* fender, as in a single item. No, we do not use front fenders. Nope, nunca, never . . . we plainly do not.

There are so many rear fenders out there to choose from, but since we are building the inexpensive way, I will start with what we use. Further on, I will also talk about finishing the fender, adding struts, mounts, and a taillight. No hurries, we are getting closer.

Let me remind you that a fender (along with other key components) can make or break your build. I can't say it enough—the lines on your bike and the flow of the components working together are essential. A fender that's either too long or too short might screw up the overall look of your build. A web of steel rods takes all the simplicity away, plus it might not be the strongest or most appealing to the eye. I'll remind you, our bike building is always a situation of less is more. Simplicity is the key. If we wanted to be comfortable, stay dry, or not get dirty, well, there's always the car . . . with an ice cold air conditioner and cool tunes on the radio.

BOAT TRAILER FENDERS

Boat trailer fenders are widely known as trailer fenders. They happen to be very inexpensive and have been a good-looking choice for decades. The mounting trick with these lies in the cutting. If you want a nice, flowing, constant arch, you will have to cut the correct length and have the proper separation from the tire. This, of course, will vary from bike to bike and depend on tire size, so it's almost impossible to give accurate information about it here. The right placement is one of those things you will have to take the time to figure out.

Most of the time, the radius of one of these fenders won't fit the tire the way we like. Of course, these fenders are made to be placed in a different way and with more separation from the tire while mounted to the rear triangle, atop and under the oil tank. Since these are bobbers and choppers, not motocross or trail bikes, we will take the time to get that fender as close to the tire as possible and with that radius looking just right.

Our favorite stop/running light for this fender is the Sparto, commonly known as the "limp dick." It looks right with flat fenders, is very inexpensive, and is easy to install. It also has a bracket for the license plate. These lights come in different finishes, such as black, chrome, or stainless, and can easily be painted any color you want.

> The radius is the curvature of the fender, which sometimes does not match with the actual wheel/tire size.

> **Tip:** We use a length of chain (530) taped along the tire lengthwise. That is our clearance between fender and tire. (Make sure the tire is fully inflated or your clearance won't be accurate. Don't laugh, it happens.) We've never had tire-rubbing problems using this method (and we sometimes fit our fenders even lower).

A view of the same gas tank. It's just a normal Sportster tank, although it has a custom Triumph gas cap from the 1970s added.

This is a normal Fat Bob gas tank, and the process of thinning it out. After it was cut and tacked, it was sent to Twisted Choppers to get finished. As you can see in the final photo, it's a pretty cool piece to use on our build. These tanks are called Slim Bobs by Sugar Bear.

MOUNTING

There are two ways we like to mount these fenders: from the cross tube behind the transmission plate mount, and from the same cross tube but above the oil tank. Mounting behind the transmission means it will be mounted full, so the bottom part (the edge pointing to the ground) will serve as a splash guard. We also use the side frame tubes and rear struts as anchor points. We tend to cut the fender at the end, almost to the fender strut mounting holes. Some are cut shorter but no longer than that.

But let's get a bit more into this whole fender mess. Mind you, the following explanation can be used for any of the fenders we use, so take note. Since I already talked about the chain length taped to the tire, we will take it from there.

We measure the frame's center, always! This ends up being a must for the rest of the assembly/fabrication work. We also measure the tire, and find the center (nope, it's never the molded center mark). We also measure at a couple of convenient spots along the frame using a string from the neck and align the marks, making sure they are straight. Once we have that center, we measure the fender's center and match them up.

A big, integral part of our builds are the fender struts. They are made simply, but they are time consuming and not as easy as they look. Here are some visual examples of how they look on our bikes:

Tip: A seamstress measuring tape is a must for all curved surfaces, and any spot that the old inflexible measuring tape won't fit. Make sure to buy one. It's a very inexpensive addition to the tool box and, like I said, it is very useful. Or simply steal it from your wife's sewing kit.

There's also a center line measuring rule available. I saw this at my friend Jay Hodge's shaping room. It works wonders to match and rematch those centers, and if you can find one in your local hardware store, pick it up.

Now that the fender is aligned and sitting in place, we bring the tire all the way forward. Maybe give the bolts a couple threads of adjustment. We start with the tire so close for a few reasons: chain stretching, fender shape, adjusting capability. The close tolerance between tire and fender won't give you much space if you screw it up. The full stretched chain should only go halfway, at the most, on the plate adjusters; the fender should still hold the proper look. I have seen people forget about this and install the fender while the axle is at center or all the way back, which shortens and/or makes impossible the adjustment later on.

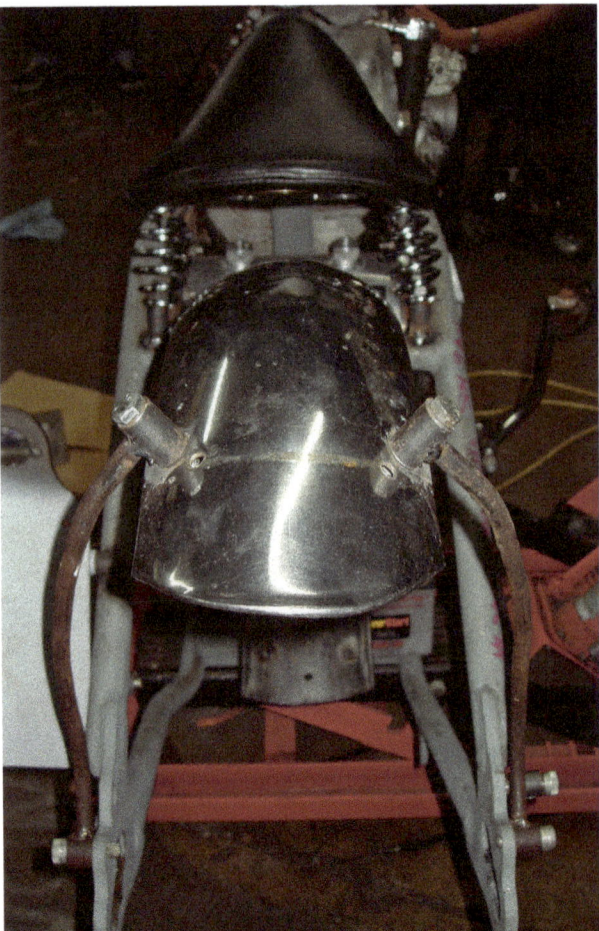

Above: *On this bike, we used a metal strap that went around the fender. I believe it looks better with flat stock than with round.*

Left: *Our struts are handmade, so they are never exactly the same (and that is the way I like it). Here's one holding an old Triumph fender, attached from above.*

These are the fender struts I made for the Indian Larry memorial bike. As you might notice, they are twisted like he used to do, and, yes, I attach most of my struts with wing nuts. I've been doing so for years.

These are very simple fender struts, with a slight bend back that you can see in their finished form.

So, once the fender is sitting where it will live from now on, we measure the space between the fender and where it will be attached to the frame. Most of the time we use metal bungs that we fabricate ourselves, so we measure from frame to fender using side bungs (mounting from the sides) or from the rear cross bar atop the oil tank, if mounting from there. (I will explain the bungs later in detail. They are super important to any job and deserve a very honorable mention.)

So once we have all these measurements, we cut the bungs to the proper length and start going at it. We mount our fender any way we like; these are just examples. Be creative but not gaudy; feel free to do whatever.

For the rear mounting we always use struts. They all have different but similar qualities. First, they are all handmade (same as our motor mounts), so no two are alike. They all have different bends, shapes, twists, or other small details.

Atop the fender, we have various anchor points. We play along as we choose or come up with new designs as the build flows, but we always (well, almost always) use the holes already provided on the frame atop the axle plates. From there, we measure toward our chosen anchor point, fix the bungs at their place with bolts, cut the rods, and get to work. We slightly tack them in place and go from there. Remember that the curves will be similar but not always the same. We need to leave room for the chain and/or the caliper.

Some people prefer sissy bars, but we seldom, if ever, use them. Here's your chance to do what you want—remember, it's *your* bike. For the sissy bar, we can get really technical using the welding table and measurements, or simply eyeball it. It's your call.

Remember that the placement of the fender is what rules. The mounts and fender struts will go wherever the fender dictates. Extreme heat does wonders to the bending qualities of metal, so measure and re-measure, fit and re-fit before the final welding takes places (or any weld stronger than just tacking).

Next, we work with the rods. Remember that you can always cut one end, and we do. We prefer the straightest side, and we always leave the rods on the longer side and grind off material for a tight fit. It's always easier to cut material off than to add it later. Remember that welding pulls, warps, and obviously moves metal parts around, so tack weld all around and always check for any movement that might screw up your work. Having the closest tolerance possible will also prevent the movement to a point.

Tip: I always take digital photos of all parts of the fender mounting as it's being constructed. Trust me, I tend to forget the way it was, or which strut is which . . . even which way is forward. You'll forget things, too. These photos are the best way to refresh your memory. No matter how good it might be, things are forgotten.

SHEET METAL

This is the mockup of the struts for the Journey Museum bike. They're the sole attachment of the fender to the bike, and they're four-point struts. They don't work for passengers.

These are very simple as well. These are in the mockup stage.

These are short and multipurpose—they also serve as the exhaust brackets besides holding the fender. I often talk about multiuse parts in this book, and this is a good example.

Some fenders are wider than others, and some have different gauges of steel. We add steel round stock and weld it around the fender lip to make it stronger. Sometimes, when we do not use fender struts, I shape the stock all around the fender, making it super strong. Once we finish and the painter does the molding, depending on the diameter stock we use, the visual effect will be minimal, much like a small spoiler. I do this on all my long choppers with wider tires, kind of as a trademark.

On this build, we are using one of Jesse James' fenders. For tires over 150, I always use West Coast Choppers' two/eight fenders. Depending on the stock size, we start from the center and start tacking. If the stock is too large in diameter, we bring out the torch and beat the metal to submission. I've made some wood patterns of the fender so I can bend the stock rod close to the fender's shape.

SHEET METAL

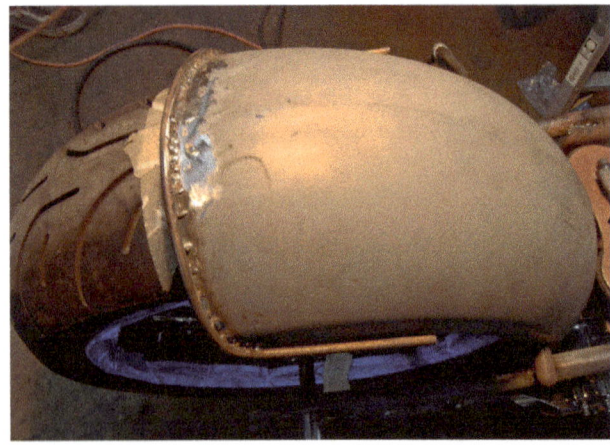

Above: *As we tack and bend it, we cut the ends off, since the bike will have fender struts. But I will also cut the round stock to meet the strut bung as close as possible*

Right: *No, I'm not going back to doing wide-tire choppers. But here's a shot of the fender before sending it to be painted.*

The finished product, paint and all. As you can see, it's hardly noticeable, but it's there, and the fender is strong. I built this chopper in 2001, beat the crap out of it, sold it, and it's still intact (the whole bike and the fender). It also gives you a kind of complete visual when the bike is done; tricks like this are what separate the really cool stuff from the normal.

OTHER FENDERS

Since the goal of a good bobber build is to use as much inexpensive stuff as possible, let's go over the rest of the fenders we use. This might give you an idea of what we use and how to find them.

Flat Fender or Trailer Fender

You can get these in any major parts catalog for about $30 to $40, or you can go to any boat supply or trailer store and get one for much less. (It might not have the radius you need, but what the hell. They are cheap, and you can always cut them up.)

'39 Ford Spare Tire Cover

Hank Young uses these all the time, and we use them, too. They are cheap, and you can cut them in half to get a couple fenders. Plus, the radius is perfect for that 16-inch tire. I really like to use them. They are mostly found at swap meets, but sadly we do not have any here in Puerto Rico. We depend on cool friends on the mainland to send them to us. You might find some online at parts or auction sites if you can't find one close to you.

Bobtail Fender

This is a very popular fender among old-school builders and a must for the Hawaiian Local Boy style. These are the most expensive of the bunch but can also found at salvage shops or in parts bins at the local shop. Remember that the best fenders are for rigids, but anything and everything can be cut up and made to fit.

Front Fenders

Nope, not the FL fenders turned ass backwards. I mean those 16-inch fenders that people take off their mega customs to look cool. You can find these fenders new at a fair price. We use the rounded ones; again, looking for that elusive radius, we cut the ears (mounting tabs) off, grind them smooth, and ready—rear fender done. Cool and unique.

We use all kinds of fenders, including this old Ford spare-tire cover. We cut up the pieces we need, and of course they're not perfect. The decades of punishment show on these parts, but they are pretty easy to fix, even if you do not have an English wheel. As you can see, the fender was dented. We wanted to make life easier for our painter, so a few quick passes on the English wheel solved that problem. We removed all the paint for easier eyeballin'. After all this is done, we will spray the fender with primer so it does not rust again and so we have a cleaner product to work with during mockup.

We can mount the rear fenders many different ways, all loosely based on the front or side mount and rear struts. When you get to this point, be creative and do your thing. It's impossible for me to explain all the ways to do this. All I know is that we try to keep it as simple as possible while being creative—no ultra-complicated criss-cross, multi-bung, multi-rod stuff (maybe you have seen them on TV). Again, to us it's the complexity of simplicity, something that works and flows is what we aim for, not some expensive ironworks sculpture.

CHAPTER 4
ENGINE AND TRANSMISSION

Most of our bob/chops start their new life with a donor bike. This means we usually have a drivetrain that has seen a previous life. We don't know how hard that life has been lived; we don't know if the engine has been well taken care of or if it's been coldheartedly mistreated. Most of the time; we have no way of finding this out, so we don't worry much about it unless we see something obvious (like a rod or pieces of a piston sticking out from the case).

Many of our donor bikes are already running, which is great and what we prefer, since at least we know they're workable. We check for leaks, fluids, exhaust, weird noises, and how it shifts and performs through the gears in general. If the motor feels strong, there's no major smoking or oil leaks, then we know we've saved a lot of time, money, and labor.

I will not lie to you, some motors we take completely apart and really go through it all, while others we just clean up and send them to the streets. This highly depends on the previous owner, the condition of the engine (discovered through experience and testing), and budget.

When we are ready to work on the engine (before taking it apart), we wash it with a solution of air conditioner cleaning acid and water. We don't use pressure hoses because we want

A side view of an empty Panhead engine case.

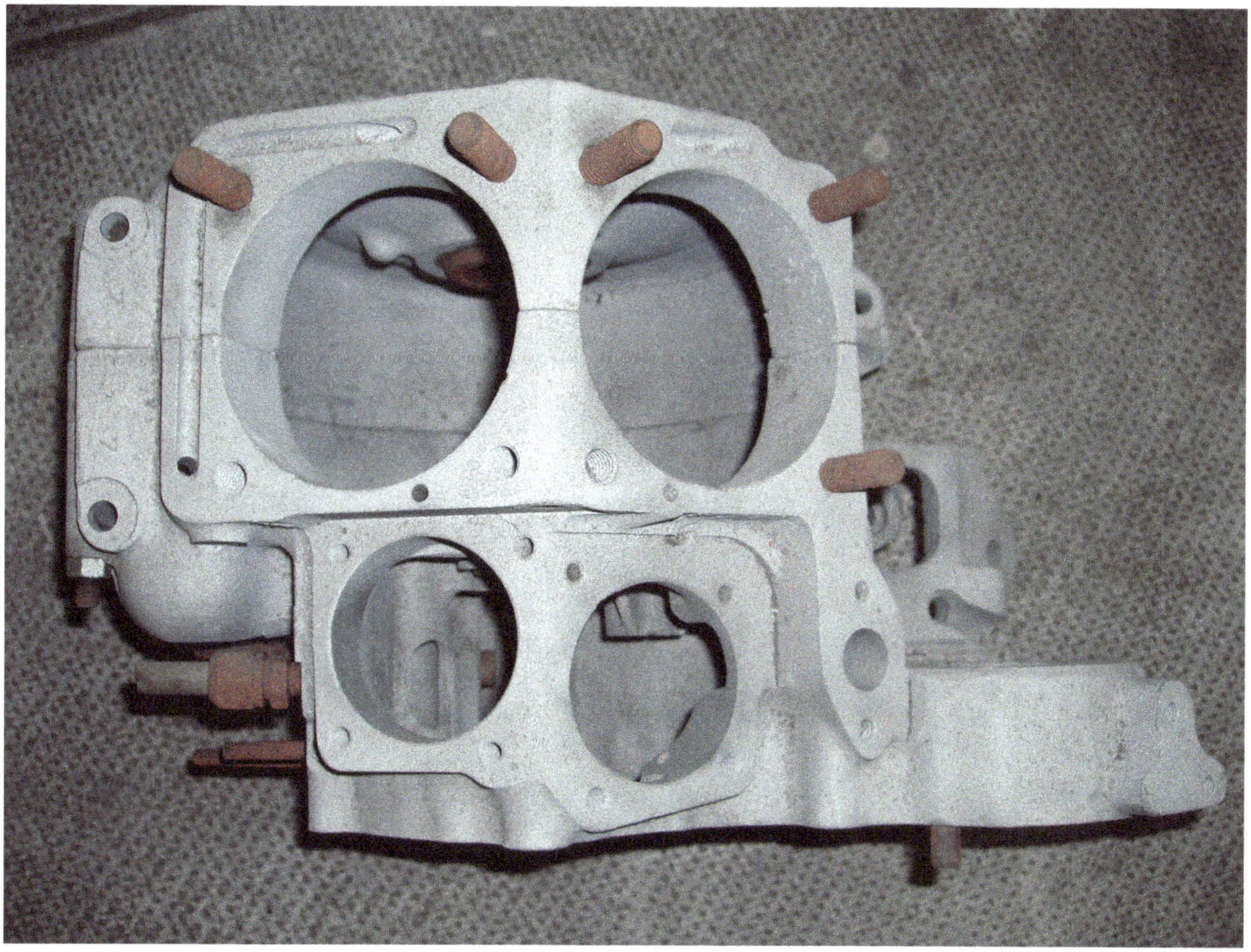

A top view of an empty V-Twin engine case (Panhead).

A view of the internals on a V-Twin Shovelhead engine being rebuilt.

A brand-new, 1200-cc Harley piston.

to avoid blowing debris around sensitive engine parts. But we try to get all the gunk and grime off. Be creative, use brushes and kitchen scrubbers, whatever it takes to get that engine really clean. It'll be easier to visually inspect the engine and will prevent problems later in the build.

When it's as clean as we can get it, we start the tear down. Every part is checked as we take it off the motor. You do what you need to do, up to your ability, time, money, or how picky you might be. Our process goes something like this:

Rocker Covers
Inspect the outside and inside for cracks, warping, and worn rocker shaft holes. Sand, polish, paint, or buy new ones (or scam them from a buddy), depending on the condition they're in.

Cylinders/Jugs
Inspect the outside and inside. Remove any paint, sandblast, and check for grooves, oversizing, or just wear from age and use. The cylinders can be resleeved if necessary. Paint them with high-temp bomb spray . . . it's cheap and protects really well. I know it's annoying when some fins are broken off, but look at it this way: those are battle scars. Age, I believe, gives a motorcycle character instead of being an imperfection.

Heads
Check and inspect the heads. If they're all OK, clean them up. If you want to be sure, change the valve seats and guides. I recommend checking and replacing them if there's any question. Oil seeping through the exhaust is not cool.

A view of bare Panhead heads.

Here are a few examples of the normal carburetors we use:

SU carbs have been around forever and work well with Evo motors, as you can see in the photo, with the manifold extension elbow.

Cases

If the flywheel feels fine (check the bearing end play), we leave it alone. Check the pistons for scuff marks (since you are already in there). If you are going to polish the pistons, then there's more to be done, but after a good cleaning we usually just consider it finished and move on.

Oil Pump

Check and inspect. You know all those comments about Harleys dripping oil and marking the spot? Most of the time, you can blame the check valve on the oil pump. Make sure to hone it properly (an old pushrod and lapping compound work great). Make sure all passages are clean and unobstructed.

This S&S Super E with a velocity stack is installed on my Panhead.

Another shot of the SU by itself.

CV carbs from Harley-Davidson are cheap and simple to find. They can be easily fitted to any engine and work fine. These are slide-type carbs, not butterfly.

Lifter Blocks
Inspect, clean, repaint, and add new seals or exchange them for new ones if necessary.

Lifters/Cam
Inspect, check for wear, bearings, etc. Check the cam for debris or obstructions close to the gears. Change the seals if needed.

Cam Cover
Inspect, polish, sand, and paint, or replace if necessary. Check bushings.

Carb
Inspect and clean thoroughly. Clean and inspect the jets, float, etc. Check the manifold for air leaks, and inspect any O-rings, seals, or bands.

After all is inspected, cleaned up, painted, polished, or trashed for a new one, we reassemble the engine using a brand-spanking-new set of gaskets (no, not the gaskets that a buddy had in a junk drawer for ages). Sometimes it's good to go with new fasteners, nuts, and bolts if you are willing to spend a bit more. We don't go all stainless steel, but we like it. Check the grade on the steel. After all this is done, finally the engine is ready to go into the frame.

Linkert carbs came on every Harley up to 1965. There is no way you can wear out one of these.

The S&S Super E is the carb to buy if you want to make your life easy. It comes complete with manifold and air cleaner, plus it has an accelerator pump for easy starting.

The S&S Super B is tuned right and will last forever. I have this one with a very cool Goodson air cleaner.

You can do this before or after the mockup. Manage your time by what's going on in the build and what you can do in the downtime. Let's say the frame is getting painted. Well, that's a good time to take care of rebuilding the engine. We try to do it whenever there's a gap in the workload, but I'd much rather do it early in case we run into problems. You know how hard it is to find stuff for pre-Evo engines nowadays. Then again, it's your time, your bike, and your call.

This is what we do with a running motor, but in many cases you will find a basket case, a nonrunning motor, or maybe just a bunch of parts and pieces. In these situations, we have to take our sweet time sorting things out, taking inventory of what we have, what's complete junk, what's missing, and what it needs. This is where praying hard comes into play.

Some more advice, even if it's not asked for: Since we are building something inexpensive, remember that the cheapest deal is not always the best. If you add and subtract repairing a whole engine versus changing gaskets, inspecting parts, and maybe changing rings, you might find out that it's better (money-wise) to buy a running bike, unless that basket case is one hell of a deal.

Compare similarities and differences between the engine at hand and what you picture at the end of your build, money-wise and time-wise.

S&S L carbs are not easy to find. This was a gift from Gennaro that I have been saving for a very special build.

TRANSMISSION

On most of our donor bikes, the transmissions are four-speed and, like the motor, heavily used and abused. A wonder of all these older Harley-Davidson transmissions is that they are virtually bulletproof, so we are on the safer side. In our case, we mostly use kickers (if not exclusively). So the first order of business is making sure the tranny has a working kicker assembly and ordering it if it's missing.

Once we open the transmission, we check all the gears, forks, and associated metal. We've found out that the forks tend to get the most abuse and are usually the culprits when something's not right.

Once all the internals are out, we clean and polish (or paint) the cases as needed. Once the outer finish is done, we reassemble with new gaskets, and it's ready to go (of course, all the other parts and fasteners get a revamping

Most of our bikes are kick-only, but once in a while we get transmissions without the kicker gear. Of course, we have to add it to them, and in the older four-speeds, it's a pretty straight-up matter (check your model's manual).

Five-into-four-speeds and five-speeds are a bit more complicated to deal with. Here, we show you the conversion of a five-speed on a four-speed case. This tranny is full of very cool Andrews gears on a Sputhe tranny case.

The part number for this item is 58290 from Custom Chrome. For five-speeds, 1987–1989, it's CCI 58291. For five-speeds, 1990–1999, it's 58291. The most common for us is the 1936–1986 four-speed kicker kit, part number CCI 25940. (Thanks to Custom Chrome for sending us this kicker kit, gratis, so you can check it out.)

We already took out the cover for a better look at the transmission trap door.

A side view of the transmission with the old shaft still in place.

CCI's kit 58290, kicker and shaft. As you can see, we have to change all the gears into the new shaft.

as well). Be sure to take special care with the shaft seal and nut since these are major areas for leaks.

OK, so you got a newer setup with a "sofatail" (no, it's not a typo) five-speed transmission (which, by the way, is also indestructible . . . well, almost), and you are wondering if you need to go through the same process. Wonder no more—we do exactly the same. We order the kicker kit and install it after we have worked the cases in and out. In these transmissions, the most damaged part is usually the fifth gear seal (burnouts, wheelies, and tight belts cause it, and we are usually guilty of at least two out of three), so we check the seal, replace if needed, and finish.

Again, all this building is within a budget. If you got a cheapo tranny from a friend or some other shady source, you have to go and inspect everything. We have seen gears, separators, and forks where they do not belong. Trust me, you would be amazed. So in this case, like others, your budget rules over the work. If you don't have the budget for the five-speed kicker kit, well, save it for later.

One last piece of advice on this: always compare. An inner primary, primary, starter, shaft, etc. all added up will be more expensive than the kicker kit. Then again, if you already have the parts, it's a no-brainer.

Top, pawls, and selector are already off.

Here's a better view of those parts; we will use them again.

Edwin is pushing away the whole gear setup, checking that everything slides out OK.

Here, you see the whole gear setup, still on the trap door.

Above: When taking the gears off, make sure you have the manual and that you place them in order as you take them off. It will make life way easier when reassembling.

Left: The empty transmission case.

Notice that a good, well-stocked toolbox and a clean working space can make life much easier.

The right tool makes the job much simpler, and that holds true in taking the clips and snap rings off.

We take the gear out with an impact tool. The kit provides a new trap door, and these old ones will go to eBay for sale.

As you're working, sort things out, everything in its place and orderly. With the daily mayhem at the shop, this organization is a totally unbelievable, shocking, sight to me.

We're ready to install the new part and add all the gears to the shaft. (Again, check your model's manual.) Assembly is simply stepping back into what you already did.

On all the bolts and stuff that come with the kit, remember to add assembly lube and anti-seize compound to everything.

Above and right: *A view from underneath and in front of the trap door being installed. Loctite all the bolts, and make sure it slides in easy. Notice that everything is very clean and the shifter selector and pawls are back in place.*

Left: Edwin slides the kicker cover in and checks again that everything fits properly. We also check if everything is shifting like it should.

Below: With the kicker cover off, we add the gasket. We do not use silicone very often; instead we use glue.

Here's a shot of the whole assembly. All that is left is to place the top cover and kicker cover back. Of course, I recommend adding transmission fluid and double-checking everything.

Here's the finished product, placed on the bike just for the hell of it. As you can see, it's complete, and some parts are still taped off to prevent scratching. After a few hours and the right tools, we have a kicker transmission.

CHAPTER 5
PRE-ASSEMBLY MOCKUP

We have talked about a lot of different steps up to this point: where to get parts, what to get, what to look for, and how to start (among other things). So here's the fun part: the first assembly or mockup. (This is where the most labor and experience is needed.)

If we did our homework right, we already have what we need or a certain idea of what we will need. Money, time, and availability are key in this process. We have a certain idea of how the bike will look as an end product. We have an idea of which front end, wheels, bars, fenders, gas tank, etc. we will use for this build. Mind you, the trick here is sticking to your guns, good preplanning, and actually having the stuff (parts) handy.

This is the way I do it, and like I have said before and will say again, it's not etched in stone. Do what you can and want to do, but these steps have worked out for me for a long time. So why not for you?

As we begin with the frame (spray bombed), we use either one of our lifts, or simply a table, or even a patch of level ground. The key word here is level. The frame needs to be level in order to start the mockup, or the end result will all be crooked. I cut 4x4 pieces of wood and metal to achieve this. Four inches off the ground will give you pretty good access to everything you need. If not, add a couple more blocks to raise the whole project.

Here is the basic frame, our wishbone rigid, with stock rake and stock stretch. We have worked with Custom Chrome to modify frames more to our liking. The frame is made for fat bob gas tanks, but we are not using them.

The grinder comes out, and Omar cuts the tank/speedometer mount. We need to have a smooth backbone and to get rid of other tabs we won't use.

Here you can see the guideline cut. We don't want to cut into the tube, so make your guideline with care.

ENGINE AND TRANSMISSION

Once it's level and secure, we tend to squeeze the motor in first. Why? Well, it's a good balance point for the frame and does not allow it to tilt forward or back (up to a point). I only drop the bolts in the mounts, no nuts or tightening, just enough so it stays in place and does not move around much or, God forbid, fall to the floor.

The motor can already be finished, checked or rebuilt, painted and cleaned up, or simply in whatever shape it happens to be in. Remember, this is the mockup. You're only checking to see how all the parts fit together. It doesn't have to look pretty, just functional.

We then install the tranny plate and tranny. We do tighten the plate but not the transmission since we will have to move it around later. Again, these are good balance points for the frame.

If you have ever done it, you know installing fork cups is a total pain. Here is an easy way to do it:

We get the fork cups in a kit, including bearings, races, and dust covers. Since taking them off is even worse than installing them, we just let them be and tape them when the frame heads to paint.

The fork cup installation tool from JIMS is worth whatever it costs. This one has paid for itself over and over again.

Left: *Here are the fork cups, neck, and tool. We lubricate the cups with assembly lube and start tightening, tightening some more, and then some more.*

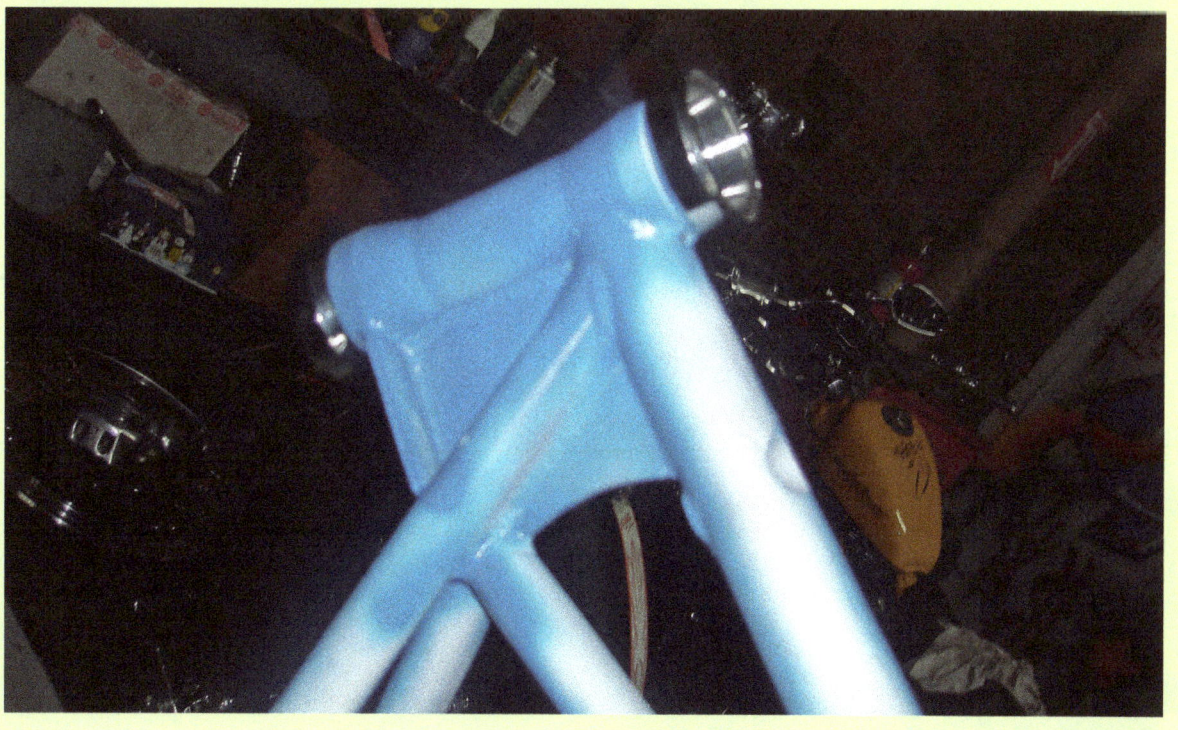

Below: *Done. Make sure both fork cups sit all the way down against the neck.*

PRE-ASSEMBLY MOCKUP

I get on the lift with the camera and shoot some more cutting, looking for maximum spark to no avail.

Before all this comes together, we have pre-installed the fork cups, so they are already in place. If you have the fork cup tool, it's a breeze. If not, some elbow grease and ingenuity will do the job.

Next, we either install the final rear wheel/tire combo (again, laced and painted, etc., or in whatever shape it's in) or I have a dummy wheel/tire combo I keep on hand for this purpose only. We tend to use the same brand of tires, so it all fits the same. Slide the axle through the wheel and frame (no hammers, please), and space the tire where it will eventually live (if you already have the spacers, brakes, and such). I have a spacer the actual size of the caliper bracket I use, so I don't get the actual caliper full of welding bits or burns. Then it's all measured up and centered.

Speaking of centered, we use a string to measure the center of the frame, from the neck back, in several spots. We get out our trusted Sharpie and mark at will. Once all the marks align, we know we have our center (since I have a mockup wheel/tire assembly, it's already centered), and we line it all up. This will be super helpful as we work, trust me. We always need to know where the center is if we want to have it all aligned.

FRONT END

Next, we move up to the front end (finished or unfinished) and slip in the bearings. As you might notice, we jumped from the rear of the bike to the front; this is just a way to keep it all balanced on our lift/table/floor.

The other side is almost done. Again, take care not to cut the tube (backbone).

> **Tip:** If you already have the front end finished, grease that bottom bearing and install; it's a bitch to get out once it's there.

Once everything is sort of tight in the front end department, we install the front tire/wheel combo (I also keep a couple on hand for mockups) and the proper spacers.

Since I don't use front brakes, we have replacement spacers for the caliper bracket if needed. We slip in the axle (again, no hammers, please), and we have a front wheel. We also install the risers and handlebars, even the headlight if it's handy.

The front wheel is the one that locks to the lift, if you have one. If not, try to secure it (straight) by whatever means you prefer. If you notice the bike starts looking like something cool, grab the camera, shoot, and save for the real assembly.

We removed the bars and risers for better clearance. The guys are removing the front fender and tire so they have better access.

PRE-ASSEMBLY MOCKUP

Since this is old stuff, a lot of penetrating oil has been added. The bottom tree pinch bolts are loosened, and the tree is pushed down into the sliders.

The whole front end is out of the bike. There are different ways of doing this. The front end shown is a 35-millimeter narrow glide. On a modern 39-millimeter, once the pinch bolts are loose, the whole leg comes off easily.

You are supposed to see the bearing. Some sucker put a wheel bearing seal in there . . . God knows why. But those are the things you find when taking apart a 1972 bike.

There's a special tool to remove the tube caps, but a crescent wrench does the job. Be careful when removing the caps—sometimes they are under spring pressure.

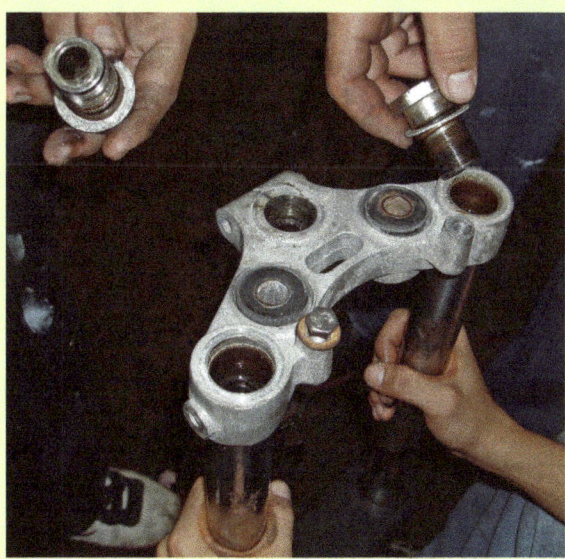

Above: *Caps are off. As you can see, the last time they serviced this front end was during Columbus' third trip. By looking at the rust on the tubes, we know the top tree will need some force to get it out. These tubes are conical, so the only way to get them out is by gently tapping them with a blow hammer or rubber mallet.*

Right: *The first slider is out. Notice the lack of grease on the triple tree axle, which caused the rust. Service on this front end was nonexistent. Repeat with the second slider.*

PRE-ASSEMBLY MOCKUP

85

PRE-ASSEMBLY MOCKUP

We just slide them in. This triple tree mounts with the axle from the lower sliding through the upper and attaches by a bolt that screws inside the axle. We make sure they sit properly, top and bottom.

Front view of the triple tree, tightened and ready for the sliders.

We use assembly lube on the tubes to slide them into the triple trees. On the Sportster setup, there are pinch bolts on the top and lower clamps, so we measure both tubes and mark them with the Sharpie to make them even, then tighten.

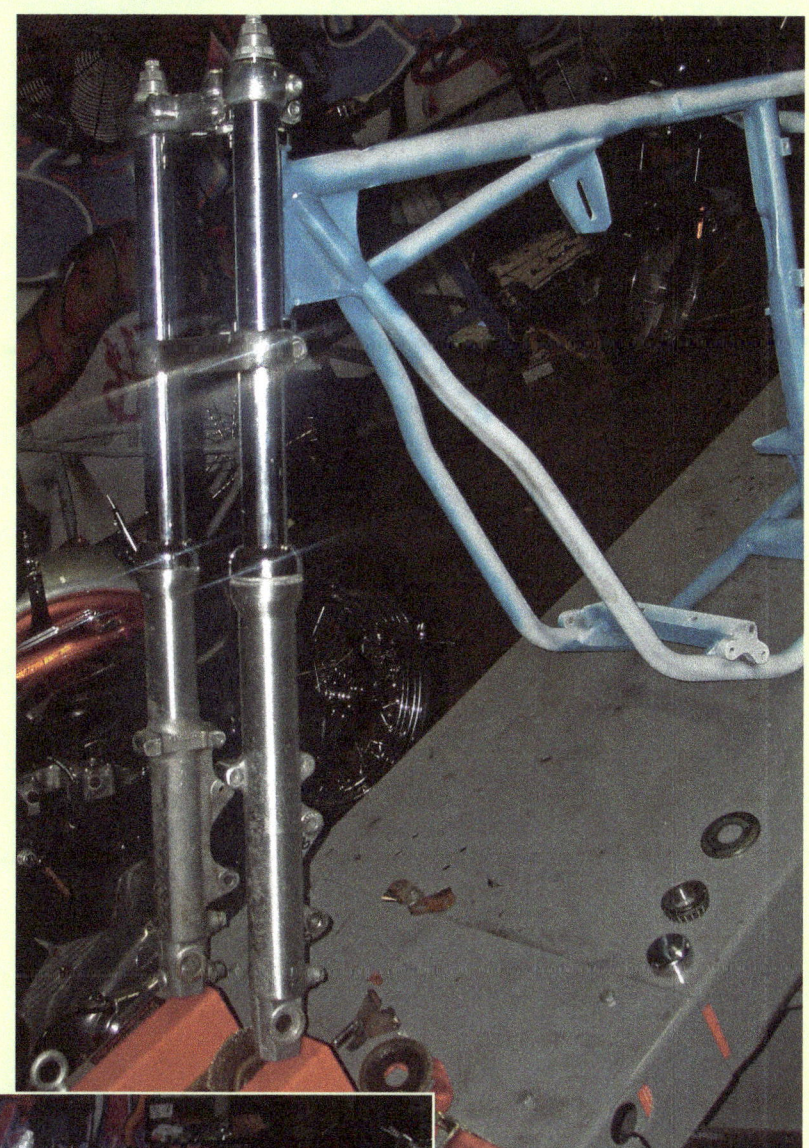

Left: With everything in place, we will now check the movement to mark where our fork stop will be, and mark everything and anything that needs to be cut off later on. I always write on the actual part, sometimes even what color it will be, or maybe a nasty note I want to leave for others to enjoy.

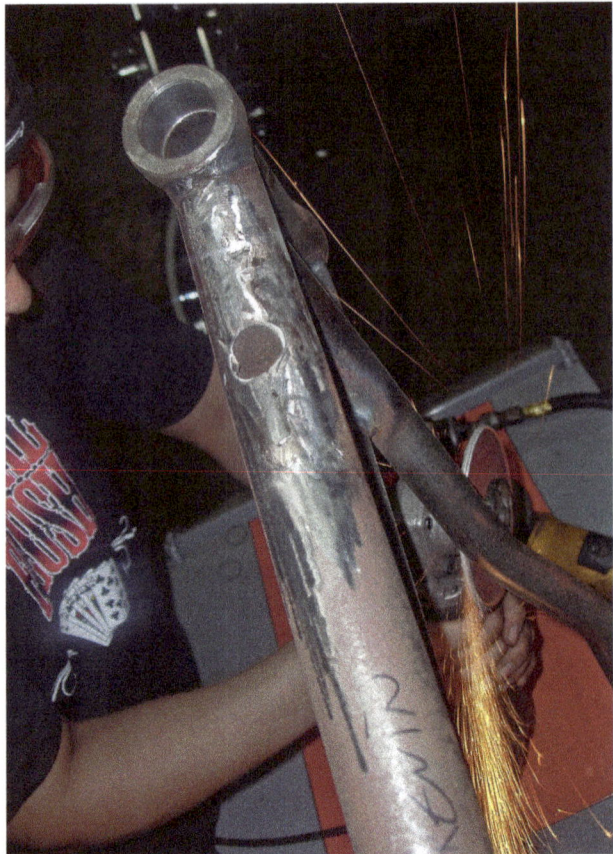

So now you see the finished cut. Waving is minimal, which will make it easier to grind smooth. Then again, plastic filler (or Bondo, as it's commonly known) will do wonders to the end product. You can also see the lower front gas tank mount has been cut off.

Above and top: *We cut the rear gas tank mounts before cutting the speedometer mount completely off for photo purposes only.*

GAS TANK AND FENDER

If we do know which tank we are using (and we should by now), or if we're deciding between several tanks, this is the time to break them out. I also place the sprung seat on its bungs just to have it there. The reality is, the more parts you have, the easier it is to take a good look at the bike and start trying to imagine the end product: lines, flow, and most important, style.

I get a rag or an old T-shirt and wrap it with tape to the backbone. This will prevent the tank from slipping and hitting the floor and also helps a lot while looking from afar to check if the position is the right one. The key word here is "afar." I leave enough space between tools, seats, toys, pool table, etc., and the bike. The best way to check the lines is to stand back and look at it from all angles. I check the gas tank, or gas tanks, until I find the setup I believe works the best or the position on the backbone that I like the most. (I keep the rag/shirt in place so all we see is the backbone, not fabric.)

Once it's in place, we grab the Sharpie again and mark where the tank sits (in the case of fat bobs, well, simply bolt them on and it's done). We look at the bike from all angles to check if it looks OK, and we also follow with measurements for the center line (although some tanks are not perfect, and measurements vary from front to back). Sometimes, the eye lets you know when it's more or less where it should be. If there's any way to secure the gas tank into position, we do so and just let it be. Sometimes I change my mind and move it a little, and that's no biggie; we all change our minds.

The frame is sprayed with rattle-can paint after being sanded off. In this case, we had a bit of white and a bit of blue left. This will prevent rusting and protect the frame from our lovely tropical weather.

As we go back to the bike's rear, I take two pieces of chain about a foot long (depending on the fender) and tape them to the tire/wheel, side by side, paying attention that I can still see my center marks. With the tire chocked, I place the fender atop the two chain pieces. (I've found 530 chains give enough clearance for the tire not to rub the fender, but some people use other stuff.) Once we align the center marks on the fender (I *did* say that you have to center it, right?) with the frame, I use welding magnets (the large ones) to keep it in place and cover the gap between the frame tubes and fender. I look at it again from all angles to see if it is what I expected, mark if I need to cut, mark the place I will attach it, and check if it's long enough for the taillight I plan on using (if it goes on the fender).

Once the fender is secure, along with the gas tank, take a good look again at how everything flows, take as many photos as you can, make any changes that you feel like making, and remember that once we start welding, it is almost (and I say almost) final.

If you already have the bungs, tabs, or any other forms of attachment for your fender and gas tank, it's time to break them out. I have all the tools I need at the shop, so I can cut them as needed, which makes life much easier. If you do not have the tools, you should have them ready at their correct lengths. (Make sure of the bolt lengths as well.)

I mark the fender for holes, mark how and where I will attach it from the front (or sides), and make as many marks as possible so that when I take the fender off, it returns to the same position it was before. Once the holes are bored, I install the bungs with bolts and also install the bottom bungs (those on the frame). Since you are working on how the struts will look (if you are using struts), move up to the front, closer to the bike, and attach them the chosen way. Once it's solid up front, it makes life much easier when doing the struts.

> I started using wing nuts in all my bikes because it made assembly a lot quicker, since sometimes parts have to come off and go back on many times. It just made my life easier. I liked how they looked and have kept using them in all my builds.

Since all the bungs are in place and the fender is solidly mounted to the front, I measure between bungs to determine the length of the rods. Twist them, bend them, or whatever rocks your boat. This will take some time to do right, and remember that the sprocket side needs clearance for the chain. Once all this is done and I can place the rods as close to the bung as possible without moving the fender; I tack them enough to hold but weak enough to break if needed. Remember that welding moves the part around and pulls to the side you are welding. Tack as much as possible on all sides (or as the space allows it).

> **Tip:** I try to weld as much as possible on the actual bike, not a welding table, because I hate surprises in the long run. You might weld a piece together on a table only to find it doesn't fit right when it goes back on the bike.

Like everything else in the build, stand back and check it out. Check if it's even, if you like the way it looks, or whatever you're concerned about. If you are happy with it, tack a bit more to make the piece stronger, and that is the end of it . . . for now.

Your rear fender should be secure. Rotate the tire/wheel, and pull off the chain you used as a spacer. The wheel should spin freely. Your wheel should be as forward as possible when you do this in order to have the most chain tension on it. Depending on the fender, the tire will look like a constant arch, more so if it's curved and has sides to it. Most fenders on the market do not fit the radius, so it becomes a pain in the ass.

If you spaced it right from the beginning, your rear sprocket should align with the transmission, and your caliper should align as well. (Don't fret if everything's not perfect. All this can be solved.)

Now that you have most of the fabrication for the fender done, move up to the gas tank. There are several ways to mount it. Most of my tanks are mounted from underneath, which is cleaner but harder to do and takes a lot of time. What I do in this case is measure the tunnel, tabs, and backbone so I know how much I have to work with. I always overmark them (it's easier to cut than add) so they are a bit longer than what I need. It takes time, but bit by bit they can be in perfect alignment to the backbone, again following the center lines and making sure the tank is not leaning more toward one side or the other.

After a long time going back and forth and getting it just right, we install the tabs on the tank, tighten the bolts, and place them atop the backbone. I use a couple metal pieces to achieve the distance I want between the bottom of the tank and backbone (if the tank sits right on the backbone it could crack). They are about 1/4 inch thick, and once I add the rubber grommets, the measurement ends up being a bit more. (Remember, paint adds to the clearance of your pieces, as well.)

Once I measure and remeasure (repeat as many times as needed), I tack the bottom of the tabs to the frame. Always check for alignment after every tack; I tend to tack in the corners in order not to pull the tab down with the weld.

Once this is done, I take the tank off and very carefully tack the top of the tab in the corners again. I place the tank back in position and double- or triple-check to see if anything moved. Once I know everything fits as I want it to, I weld the tabs.

SECOND GAS TANK SCENARIO

There are some gas tanks that already come with flat tabs front and aft. If you decide to go this way, drill a hole where the tank will be attached to the backbone. I mark them with the tank in place, go back to my lathe, and make a couple bungs (whatever diameter you choose; it's up to you). Drill and tap them for the bolt you're using (usually 3/8 inch), drill the backbone, insert the bung (leaving the space for clearance needed), and weld it to the frame. This will give you a strong attachment point, better than just drilling the frame and getting two or three threads gripping the bolt at the most, and it makes it stronger.

I tend to measure the tube depth and make the bung a 1/4 inch longer or so. The attachment (anchor points) on these gas tanks will be forward and aft, so we just repeat the process. So far, this method has worked very well. We also add some rubber washers to dampen vibration a bit.

THIRD TANK SCENARIO

If we are using the stock mounts, we always Frisco our gas tanks (to keep alignment with the backbone angle). We measure the height on the front, all depending on the depth of the tunnel and mount, and if it will fit well. (Most of the older XL gas tanks do, but the modern ones suck.) I cut a piece of metal that will fill the gap between the bung and backbone. Once we have measured between tank tabs and fabricated the bung with threads on both sides, or just drilled from one side to the other, we go toward the back and mark (remember the spacing from the backbone). Proceed to another bung (like the ones used in the previous tank scenario) that will go thru the backbone. Tacked in place, the bolt goes through, and we tack the front bung and stock metal spacer. We check for everything to look OK, and proceed to tack stronger.

I've given you three scenarios, but there are (and will be) many others. These are the most common and the ones we use. Once the tank is fairly secure, we can stand back and check our work. Again, take plenty of photos of everything and anything. Digital cameras rule, as you can delete later whatever you don't want. But I tend not to delete. I never know when the weird shot with the guys monkeying around in the background will be needed.

Once we have this sort mockup, we will move to the oil tank and motor mount. This is how I put together my bikes, but anyone can buy a motor mount, tighten a couple bolts, and voila! I prefer to fabricate my own.

When I was building the Journey Museum bobber, I noticed that none of the actual period bobbers had barrel oil tanks; they were all horseshoe. I had a couple of modern Softail oil tanks around the shop, so I decided to do a different version of them. In this case, time was crunching big time, so after I mocked up what I wanted, I sent it to my friends at Twisted Choppers in South Dakota, and they got the job done in record time. That's what friends are for, and it left time for me to work on other stuff.

I cut the tank in half and removed about an inch on each side. I had to make them match, so I worked on them until they kind of lined up. It's badly tacked but holding together.

As you can see, it's badly tacked all around, but it's the shape I want.

The Twisted Choppers tank, with different mounts and oil cap. It fits perfectly.

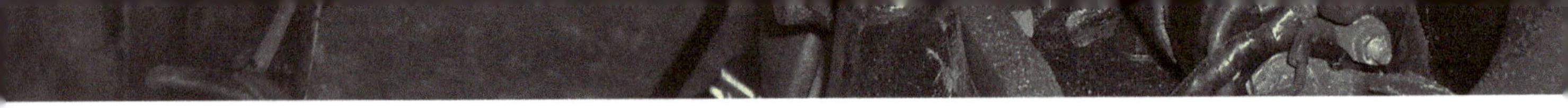

PRE-ASSEMBLY MOCKUP

A top view of how the oil tank will fit.

A look at the raw finished oil tank. I still cut a few brackets and made new ones. As you can see, it looks bitchin'.

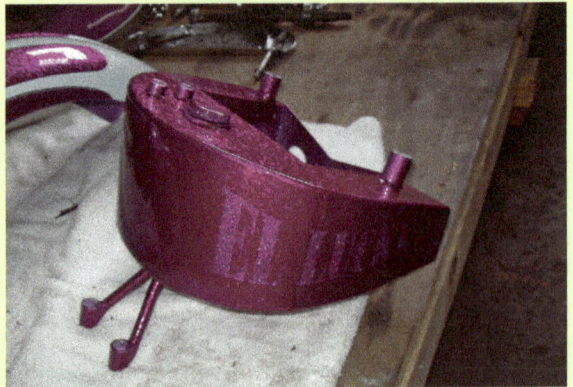

After paint and all the brackets were finished, I really liked the end product. If I had more time, I'd finish the whole job myself. You'll probably do it yourself. This is one of those very inexpensive changes that will make your bike stand out.

OIL TANK

In order to continue our assembly mockup, we will follow the transmission installation with the oil tank. There are different oil tank styles we can use. Most of my oil tanks are barrels (the horseshoe style is a pretty straightforward mount, unless you get creative and cut everything up), so most of my tabs and bungs are the same kind of setup.

My friends at Twisted Choppers in South Dakota fabricate most of my oil tanks, so I send them the measurement I need for the frame I plan to use (remember: pre-planning). The installation is pretty straightforward: cut the tabs to length, place the oil tank where it should be, etc. But before doing this (and this applies to any oil tank you might be using), check for clearance with the top of the transmission, the clutch lever, and the jockey shift lever. We also place the coil if it's going near the oil tank. It's a good idea to bolt on everything you might imagine could interfere once the oil tank is mounted and check for clearances.

The reason I left the transmission unbolted is so I can slide it forward and back until I find the right spot where it won't come in contact with anything. Other parts can be bent and fabricated and relocated, but when the transmission is in place, you're pretty much stuck. Once the tranny is tight, the travel should be minimal (but then again, you never know).

Before tacking, remember to measure, again and again, making sure everything is straight and level. Mind the oil tank outlets and their fittings. Also keep in mind that the oil tank will be a bit offset, since one side has the fill hole (unless it's in the center). Once everything seems fine, tack the tabs in the corners in order to reduce movement during welding, strong enough so it stays in place.

In case the oil tank also has a back bracket, a piece should be fabricated in order to bolt it with four anchor points. When the battery goes into the oil tank, it is recommended to use the four anchor way.

I have used a lot of tanks with many different styles and configurations, and I fabricate or move stuff as needed, whether it's the fill neck, mounts, outlet holes, etc. Of course, you are building your own bike, so you will discover the best way to do it.

I am jumping a bit ahead here, but once we remove everything (transmission, motor, and such), I try to tack the bottom of the oil tank tabs *before* taking the tank off. Again, this will lessen the movement by welding pull.

I have mentioned the four-point mounting system, because this is sort of what the factory does. Again, we have made those brackets in many different ways, sometimes using them to also hold the seat springs or the rear fender. I create bungs, tabs, and attachments to be multipurpose, making my life difficult to keep the bike simpler.

So now that we have the oil tank in place, I tighten the motor, transmission, etc. (Remember to tighten the rear engine bolts first. This is an old trick: If there's any clearance in the front mounts, shim and then tighten. An aluminum can does wonders for shims.)

PRIMARY AND MOTOR MOUNTS

If you do have the primary, or are using an enclosed primary, go ahead and bolt it. This will give you the right spacing between motor and transmission. When we start working on the motor mount, I prefer doing my own motor mounts; they are simple and efficient. I do not hang anything extra from them, no coils, no switch, no choke. The first chore is taking off those pesky studs. Sometimes they have been living there for decades and tend to get a bit stubborn. The lucky one will get them out right away, while others might have to be very creative. (I've had to tack weld a nut to the stud and wrench it out several times.) If it comes out right away, lucky you. Once these are out, we have to tighten the bungs and bolts.

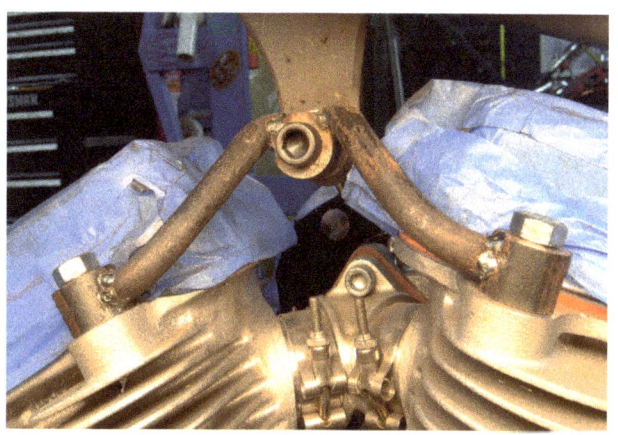

As you can see here, we hand fabricate all our motor mounts. You'll need three bungs and some round metal stock. None of the mounts are the same, although they're all similar. All the bends are handmade for each bike.

The finished mount for one of my choppers. This one looks like the beefiest of them all, yet it's the only one that cracked. I did not weld it right; I was in a hurry and was late. Then again, it was fixed and is still working.

Here are some ideas for mounting the oil tank. Sometimes I need to improvise and work with what I have and fabricate the mounts, since our oil tanks are seldom mounted the way they were intended.

We cut this tab to attach the oil tank up top. Notice the notch so we can reach the oil cap. This had to be done because the space was very limited. This specific oil tank took over ten labor hours to make it work right.

I had to come up with this mount in a cross pattern to hold the oil tank. Sure, I will have to move the fittings and fill hole, but it will work and look funky when finished.

This bike's owner worked with me to make an oil tank out of a truck's exhaust pipe. I fabricated the straps and welded them to the tank. People really like this tank, but I doubt I will do it again.

Another example with different bends.

This is how the motor mount looks after being ground, molded, and painted.

PRE-ASSEMBLY MOCKUP

This is the motor mount for the Chop-Off bike. The metal is twisted like Indian Larry used to do. Mara Plating did the bronze plate, and I sanded it to remove the shine.

You need two bungs for the bolts that go into the heads and a larger diameter bung that goes into the engine mount bracket in the frame. Choose the appropriate-sized bolts for the job, and tighten away. (I have used the top bung to also hold the carburetor in place by the manifold.)

On the top bung (the one that goes into the frame), I tend to add a washer to give it some space. This allows room for the paint, and you can always add it at the final assembly if needed.

Once all this is done, I choose the stock I intend to use. Depending on what we are doing, we might use twisted metal, round stock, or something else. I try to plan out whatever I am doing before starting the motor mount. Mostly I use round stock, determine its correct length, and bend it in a U shape with the tube bender (or anything else I can find). Unless the bends are going to be tricky or complicated, I just bend it cold.

Once I have something close to what I want, I cut two pieces out and start working on the mount. Placing the pieces in different positions until they fit takes some time. I grind grooves in them so they come as close as possible to the bungs without touching the heads. Once I am happy with it, I tack weld them down. Remember that they won't be the same length. You'll notice a stock motor mount has slots to be able to move them around—these won't.

Once everything is tacked and looking good, cover the motor (if you did not do it already) and tack some more, or simply weld away. Again, it's better to weld stuff in position. After this, all it will need is some more welding, some grinding, and it's ready for the paint booth.

All of the above steps are the minimal mounting fabrication that you might do, but like they say in infomercials, just wait . . . there's more.

EXHAUST BRACKETS

If you are using a custom exhaust, or simply want some trick brackets, you've got to do them yourself. We hold the pipes in place by different methods. The most important thing to remember is to install the pipes where they'll sit once it's finished. Front and rear, check the clearance on the pipe against the brake caliper or anything else back there (like the axle and adjusters), and check for clearance on the kicker leg, oil tank, and anything else near the front of the pipe. By

This finished mount is from the Journey Museum bike.

now, you should have most of the bike mocked up, and everything that you will use should be bolted in place. I'm not talking about every single part (coils, switches, controls, primary, kickstand, etc.) since there are too many variables from build to build. But knowing where everything will be helps a ton, style- and fit-wise.

If you decide to be brave and fabricate your own exhaust, the way I do it is by using existing pieces of exhaust. I make a sort of diagram (sucky drawing, really) of the way I want the pipes to go. I measure, eyeball, and cut as needed. Each piece is tacked in place, again, making sure it is all straight.

Making your own exhaust is simpler than you might think, although very time consuming. If you do have pieces of pipe lying around, you are golden. If you don't, it's another story. Then again, they do sell tubing with the bends already made and such, but the goal is an inexpensive build.

When I do my own pipes, I tend to drill a hole at the back end of each, far enough so you can't see the bolt but close enough that you can reach it with a wrench. As I fabricate the mounts, the bolt will go through the pipe and into the bracket. That keeps things looking clean.

STARTING SWITCH AND TOGGLE SWITCH

This is pretty simple and straightforward. I look around for a good place to put the starting switch. Since we stick to kickers only, all we need is an on/off switch. Although the shapes are all the same, I tend to keep it close to the oil tank since most of my electrical stuff will be back there. I also try to keep the toggle switch close to the start switch for the same reason. Sometimes, we use the headlight housing (which is common for my bikes). That way, there's only one wire coming back to the electrical cluster from the light.

Most parts catalogs have a switch bracket available. They are pretty inexpensive, and they come with two holes for bolting on. I cut them up and weld them to the frame (making sure there's nothing close to the switch). And lucky for us, the bolt holes are big enough for the toggle switch, so I cut it off and weld it as well. I try not to do the same thing twice, but these parts all end up in similar places. They cost five bucks, and you end up with both tabs and money well spent.

The other common way to mount the switch on my bikes is right on the oil tank battery bracket. I just drill a hole into it and install. Again, since we use kickstarters only and

Left and above: *Different ideas for mounting the key switch.*

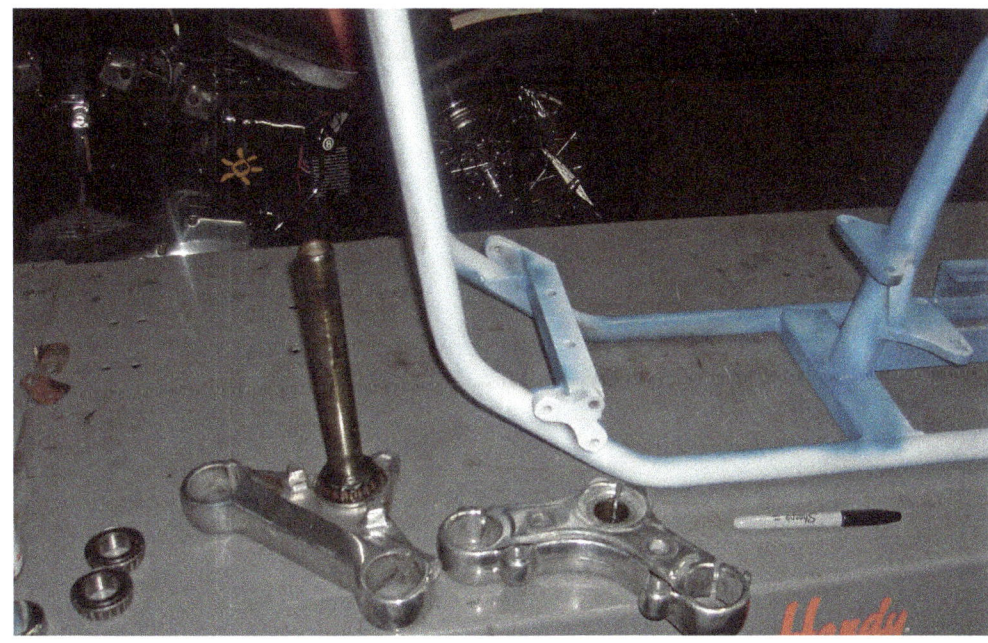

Here we are installing the mockup triple tree (in this case, a modern 39-millimeter Sportster front end). We scored this used front end, and we will keep the lower tree bearing for the mockup. As you can see, we have the new bearings for use later on. Also, our trusty Sharpie pen is handy to mark things, such as where to cut the stops.

Another angle of the triple tree on our handy lift.

minimal lighting, we get away with using very small batteries, so I have more than ample space to do this and still fit the battery. That cleans things up, big time.

FOOT CONTROLS

If you are using forward controls, that's a pretty straightforward mounting. Just bolt them on there. The only trick here—if your frame does not provide for floorboard mounts and you want floorboards—is that you will have to fabricate or buy the mounts. They're available in any parts catalog. You will need the floorboards, floorboard mounts, and frame mounts.

I install the front part of the floorboard, all the other brackets, and make sure they are level. The frame brackets need to be cut to size. Once that's done, I simply tack them to the frame as well as I can and re-tack them once the floorboards are placed where they need to be. Again, they should be level and aligned.

Double-check the right side for pipe clearance. There are also some brackets available if you are using drag pipes in certain bikes.

CHAPTER 6
DISASSEMBLY

After all the work of putting the whole thing together, fitting and matching all the parts, the time comes to take it all apart for final finish. This may include cutting and grinding parts that need it, finishing welding the frame and other parts, painting and chroming, and whatever else needs to be done.

Since most of the parts have been tacked, such as tabs, struts, and other fasteners, I always take the time to weld them properly once the whole mockup is taken apart. If you did your homework when organizing the build, you'll have a list of what needs what. A very important tip mentioned earlier is to take as many photos as you can, since these will become very handy later on when we do the final assembly.

To simplify things later, start marking what is what. Ziploc bags are a great way to organize bolts, washers, and nuts. Get the trusty Sharpie and write it down. All the markings you made to cut or grind on the frame and other parts will pay off here.

This is the last step before everything goes to paint. The oil tank, sliders, rims, hubs, frame, fender, struts, and license plate bracket are the first things you'll want to work on. You'll have time to redo the motor (as needed) and transmission, work the triple trees, cut the slider tabs, upholster the seat, etc., while the tin is being painted. This is the time to do all those things you listed before the build began. Remember to work on the things that will go to paint first, trying to send the whole package to the paint shop together. No one likes having most of the parts but not being able to put the bike together because some parts are still at the painter.

The ideal situation would be that once the frame is in, you start working and assembling right away. We run a shop, so we try to maximize our time from build to build. All these actions take place with several bikes going on at the same time. When you do it at home, pace your time at your convenience.

So you are looking at your final mockup of what your bike will look like. This is, again, a great time to take as many photos as possible. To me, the coolest part of the whole build is when you look back at those photos and compare them to the final product, like Frankenstein becoming one of those babes in a beer commercial. Most of the people who come into the shop are not able to visualize what the bike will become, so photos of finished bikes are a great way to illustrate it. To them, it seems impossible that a bunch of rusted metal can become what they see in the end.

I do not go on a frenzy and start taking everything off the frame. I tend to take notes on what needs to be ordered, which bolts we need, etc. Since we have all our parts marked up already, notes about them go on the list, as well. I write down right on the part what needs to be done. Since those notes will be painted over during final assembly, the hard copies will be my guide when it all comes together. Try to safely save and organize all the parts that belong to that bike (when this is your only project, it's much easier) so you don't get a mix-match of stuff in the end.

I built shelves in front of my lifts to hold whatever parts belong to that certain bike. Well, at least that was the plan. It probably lasted a couple months. When you have bikes on and off of the lifts all the time, it just becomes extra storage for stuff. A good tip is to buy or build a shelf dedicated to your build. They are available all over. I also keep a bunch of plastic bins in different sizes, and they work wonders. The hardest part of a build is keeping your stuff organized and knowing it will be there when needed.

Remember, just because the bike is going for paint, it doesn't mean you can take a break and forget about the whole project. Believe it or not, it's the details that kill you. As I mentioned earlier, this is a great time to work on the engine and transmission while they're both off the frame. As I take apart a mockup, I tend to reverse the way I put it together. If you have help, you can do this very quickly.

I start working on the frame as soon as it's bare, as well as anything that needs to go to the painter. I do this because painting is normally the step that takes the longest, so the quicker it gets to the painter, the better. Also, taking time grinding all the welds and making it as smooth as possible will save time at the painter's.

I also take the time to cut off anything that won't be used, making sure it's actually stuff I don't need before cutting. I prefer to cut brackets and tabs that aren't being used, but if you plan on future changes and you might use them later, you might want to keep them. One pair of brackets I have the hardest time cutting off is the forward control tabs. Because I use mid controls, there's no actual need for them, but you never know when things will change and you will want them. Another trick is to come up with something that hides them, like oil filters and kickstands. My frames have several of the tabs I need already built into them, but all builds are different, so I sometimes end up with extra brackets. I cut them as clean as possible and save them (you never know when they will be needed again), then grind the frame smooth.

Once all the extra tabs are gone, I fire up the welder once more and start welding all the parts that we already tacked. Like I said, I prefer welding the parts right where they belong, and I try to do it while time allows. Remember, everything needs to be welded well, whether you're using TIG or MIG. If you are not up to the task, please hire someone who is. It's your ass in the long run, and I mean that in many ways.

I try to make every weld as clean as possible, even when I'm tired, or bummed, or I know the waves are pumping and I am stuck at the shop. I know the cleaner the welds (visually and structurally) the less grinding will be needed, hence, less time spent getting full of metal dust.

Once a tab is in place, I tend to fit the part over it or attach it once more and give it a check. The gas tank, rear fender, and oil tank are on the top of the list (in that order).

This is also a good time to add stuff to the bike. I have welded rods down the backbone to match the gas tank, drilled holes, added tubing to the frame, hidden electrics, regulators, etc. Just simple ideas that come up late at night, almost unnoticeable but that (to me) adds quality to your work.

Hank Young is the master of this stuff. He creates around the bike and sits there until he gets it right. To me, besides being one of my very good friends, he is the master of detail. He will never be rich (way too many hours spent on each bike), but damn, his work is sacred to him. And that's better than money. All his bikes have some very tricky stuff added from cars or boats or wherever.

I am a total freak for things that look clean, stuff that is hidden and can't be seen, and stuff used in a way it's not supposed to be. But this all takes time to figure out. There's nothing worse than hiding all the wiring inside tubing and then later having to check it or troubleshoot it. Trust me . . . it will suck. Have a clear plan of attack before you hide wires or weld something where you won't be able to reach it later.

Mike Maldonado, one of my good friends and a fellow builder, is one of the best. And up until now, he has built the cleanest bikes I've ever seen. Many of those trick parts you use today were made by him first, including inverted front ends, single-side swingarms, single-side pulley/brake combos. Yeah, Mike started those. I would meet him at all the shows, and we'd dissect his newest build. Although his style is way different than mine, he is a big influence.

When I talk about a great build, I use the word clean and not perfect. I do not believe in perfection. Only God and machines can accomplish that, and we happen to be mere mortals. I also believe that a bike must have some flaw, however minimal, and it does not matter where. It just shows that an imperfect human made it and not a machine.

So your frame is totally done, all the welding, grinding, etc. Or at least, you think it's done. Give it a last once-over before heading for paint. Remember, this is your last chance before you can't work on it anymore (without removing the costly paint). Then again, don't dwell on it too much, or the frame will never leave your shop/house.

The rear fender is no big deal. If you are using a fender brake light, make sure the holes are drilled. Make sure the fender is cut for the chain or any other places it needs to be cut. (Give enough space for that chain to slap around.) I've used metal rod stock to reinforce the fenders, especially the rear lip (which has a tendency to crack under vibration). Heating the rod will make life easier, or, depending on the diameter of the rod, it can be bent by hand and tacked as you go. I've made fenders with rods running down the center, or maybe a flat bar. You need to do all this before paint, of course. And again—I can't repeat this enough—make sure everything is straight and level. A good way to check that the curvatures of the fender and rod or flat steel bar match up is to get some welding rods from the TIG welder and bend them by hand and use them as a guide. I create welding jigs on my table all the time to help with tasks like this. More or less, your fender will be ready for paint after it's been strengthened a little.

I try to do everything I can to the gas tank before I start fitting it, since I know which one I will ultimately use. The only reason for this is so it can go to paint with all the other metal parts at the same time, quickening the job. Checking the tank for any leaks is very important.

Pressure testing is a must, and I've created a special cap for this step. Drill a hole in the plastic fake cap that comes with the tank and run an air hose fitting through it. Fifteen to twenty pounds are more than enough, and with soapy water and a rag or sponge, you can search for any air bubbles. Be glad if there are none, and if by any chance there are, mark them, weld, and repeat.

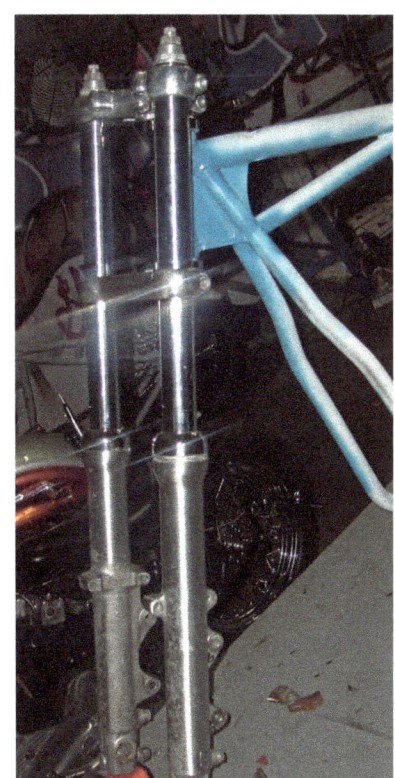

These are the sliders that we mostly use. They are take-offs from Sportsters or Dynas. Most people take these off to go for the Wide Glide look. Suckers. Their loss is our gain. We'll take this to our local machine shop buddy and have him shave the fender mounts and brake mount. The machine turning leaves them pretty smooth and kind of saves us some work.

After being shaved, see how much cleaner they look? And leaner too. After this, we will pass them on for polishing or painting.

If you are painting the wheels or the fork sliders, now is a good time to get them ready, as well. No worries if you're not ready. If your painter is anything like Pepo Paint (my painter), they will be mudding the frame and sheet metal for some time. My painter will always let me know when he's about to spray, so I know if I have to hurry and get the parts ready.

Before sending all the parts off, get them organized and make sure to pack them according to paint color, coating, chrome, etc. It never hurts to make a note of what should be black, white, and chrome just to avoid surprises and grief later on. Once everything is gone, I start working on the front end and wheels (since I paint them all) so I can have them ready in time.

Once the front end is apart, I take the tubes and sliders to the band saw and cut the fender and caliper tabs as close as possible. Sometimes you can get away with grinding the sliders smooth since paint will cover the part, but we also send it to the machine shop to get a good close shave. Once the tabs are off, we disassemble the sliders/tubes if they are going to the lathe or if we suspect they are bent. We drain the old fluid no matter what, and if we suspect that the tubes are bent (and it's not obvious), we roll them on a flat, level surface. Trust me, you will notice the bumps. If it's all OK, we just send them to paint and reassemble.

The triple trees might be painted, polished, or something else. Some triple trees you can take completely apart, but others you can't. Time to take off that pesky bottom bearing and find out. I go back to the band saw and cut anything that I won't use. A lot of grinding, a ton of patience, and some polishing will mostly do the trick. I slowly grind them to the shape (or close to the shape) I want, drill for the headlight, and by then they are mostly ready to go back on the bike.

Again, one man's trash is another man's treasure. People dropped these Sportster/Dyna triple trees like they had the plague, so they're easy to find. And these are exactly what we use for our builds.

Here they are after a good close shave with the band saw and some grinding.

Here's a set of factory triple trees, already worked.

Don't forget to pack those bearings well, and don't forget to grease the axle. I tend to forget the fork stops, so here we go. There are fork cups that do serve as internal fork stops, but I have also used chains or simply the lower tree working with the frame as it was intended in stock configuration. But my preferred way is by welding a tab of metal stock on the neck. (If you see modern Sportsters, their stop is kind of what I am talking about.) The best way to do it is to measure how far the front end will go before stopping. Once I have that measurement, I cut the metal piece accordingly. If it's all clear, I tack and check all over again. Sometimes those aluminum tabs on XL front ends are gone, and I have to cut, drill, and tap for a 3/8-inch Allen bolt, which works very well. This is another part of the build where you can figure something out, something that works and looks cool or, best of all, something you can't see at all. For now, my preferred method is to use internal stops. Although they cost a bit more money, they are invisible and they work.

I try to do as much as possible during this part of the build. There's nothing worse than assembling your bike after painting and noticing that you forgot something. It does and will happen. Knowing what you want, what you need, and what needs to be done is the most important part. (Even as I write this, I have a pad next to me jotting down notes of stuff that needs to be addressed, and I know I will forget things.)

ENGINE AND TRANSMISSION

This might be a good time to dig into the heart of your bike. As it is in pieces, we can check everything mechanical. Assuming they're in good shape, clean the cylinders with some paint remover solvent and repaint them with high-temperature spray paint. I shy away from powdercoating or any other kinds of coatings, simply because the cylinders need to breathe by expelling heat, and most coatings hamper this. Plus, if it's chipped, powdercoating can't be touched up. Old cylinders and heads have a porous surface and oil has seeped into them as years have gone by. This leads to other coatings flaking off in the long run.

I do not use sandblasting very much. Although the parts end up looking bitchin', it makes them more porous and they tend to get dirtier later on. On aluminum alloy parts, a good solution of water and air conditioner acid will do the trick. With sandblasting, you have to take everything off the heads and wash thoroughly afterward. It's a pain.

The rocker boxes are another story. They can be polished, painted, engine turned, brushed flat, or any other cool finish idea you can come up with. I do not recommend chrome for the same reason I don't recommend powdercoating. On an older engine, it's just going to flake off eventually. Trust me, I see so many bikes, and it's always cool to see something different. And remember, different does not equal gaudy.

The cam cover is made of the same aluminum alloy as the engine cylinders. It can be cleaned with the same water/acid solution and polished, painted, etc. Again, there are plenty of things that can be done to it. As I write this, I am searching for different treatments on metal and will try them out . . . you never know. Maybe simple accents, bronze, brass, black, etc., will help your overall finished look. A scuff pad can leave a pretty cool finish in any shape or pattern; try out some creative ideas.

Change the brass bushing on the cam if needed before returning the cover to its place. Double-check the cam and gear alignment, check for any debris around the area, and please remember to add a new cam bearing.

DISASSEMBLY

As we take apart the donor bike, we have to get rid of the primary in order to access the motor and transmission. The process is pretty straightforward (check your manual if you have doubts), but removing the hub needs a bit more time . . . and a hub puller.

There you go—the whole view of the '72. We have removed the primary chain, since it's not a complicated process, and the hub nut is out for a better view. (Remember, it's a reverse thread.)

A close-up of our task at hand.

Some of the tools and the hub puller.

This tool is multiuse. In three-bolt and five-bolt hub configurations, it fits a variety of applications.

DISASSEMBLY

Impact tool time. In this case, it's electric and makes the job much easier than a ratchet. The hub spins, and the impact tool compensates for its spinning.

Side view of the puller. We use the same hub stud nuts to hold the tool in place.

Above: *The hub is out. Now it's time to get to the woodruff key.*

Left: *Keep in mind the woodruff key has been there for some time, so it will be a hard sucker to get out. By the look of the maintenance on this bike, we were pretty sure it was frozen there (and we were right).*

Once the inner primary nuts are loose, the inner primary is free to come out.

DISASSEMBLY

Now it's time to remove the engine and transmission. It's just a matter of loosening four bolts on the motor and five on the transmission.

There's no such thing as a suicide shift. The proper name is suicide clutch, since it kicks back when your foot is not pressing it (like a car).

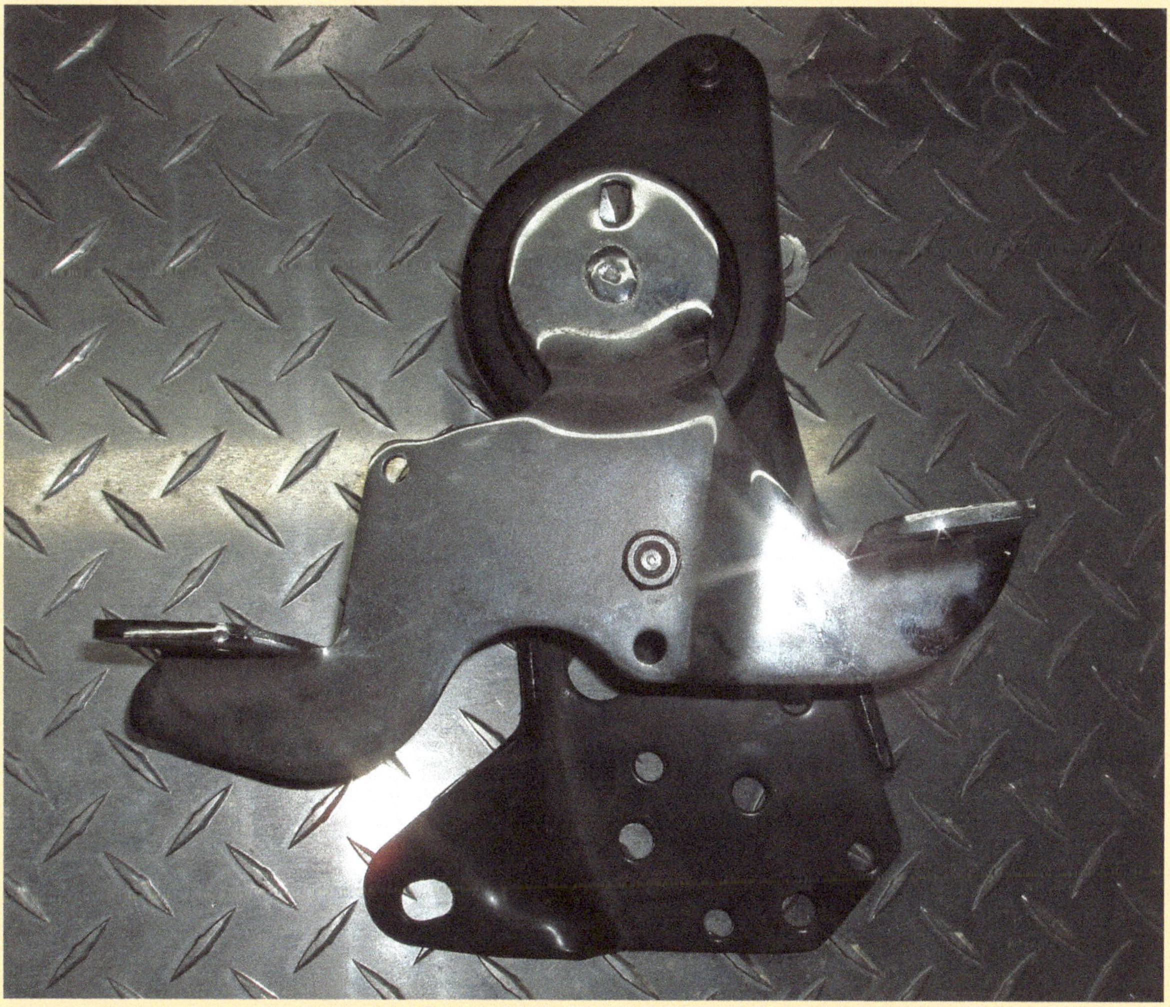

A rocker-style clutch. This clutch stays whether it's engaged or not, very common on all hand-shift stock bikes.

This is what we fabricate to use a foot clutch with modern-style forward controls.

DISASSEMBLY

Here's a quick example of the start of a handmade clutch . . . a foot clutch, of course.

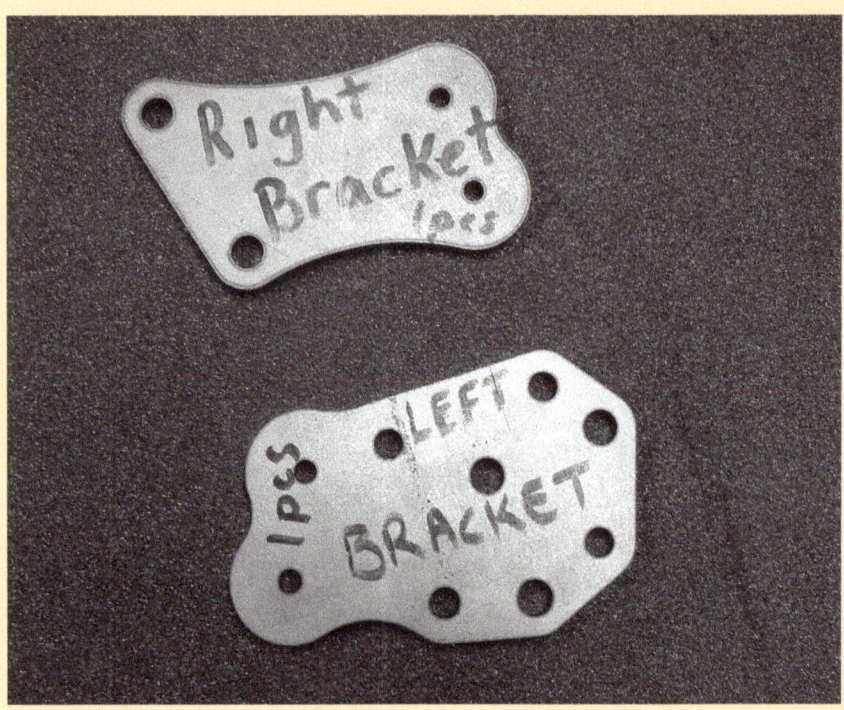

Fabricator Kevin sent me these plates, and they worked perfectly for what I had planned. He has them available for any kind of setup.

Above: A top view of how I attached the heim joint and clutch cable to the lever. I welded a piece of round stock and threaded it so I could fasten the setup with a nut. The cable is actually a broken piece of clutch cable—recycling at its best. I welded a stop so the lever does not kick all the way back.

Left: I had already twisted the lever and bent it accordingly. Also, the bung was welded to the lever and bolted. I did the brake lever in a similar way.

A side view of the whole setup actually working. One of these days I'll get around to painting them—they've been like this for two years now.

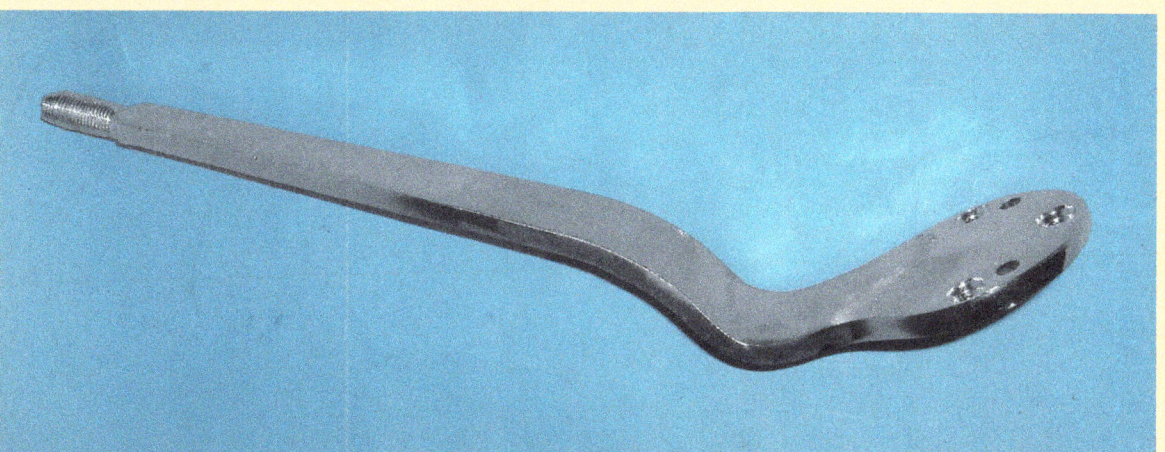

These regular levers are made for ratchet-top transmissions. We bend them according to each bike, to clear the oil tank, and coil position.

Most of our bikes are shifted by hand. Jockey shifting is the way to go. It's simple and functional. Here are some examples of various levers:

Our fabricator, Kevin, made this lever for what's called the "cow flop" transmission. He's the only one I know who does this conversion kit. Here, you can see it installed in the bike and bent to clear the oil tank and coil.

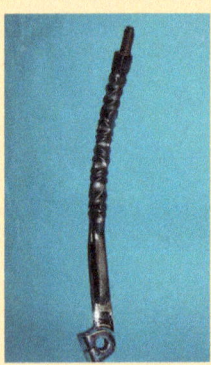

Above: *I did this Indian Larry–style twisted shifter for a five-speed transmission.*

Right: *Another shifter on a five-speed 'Softail-style transmission.*

Above: The first twisted lever, which I made for the Journey Museum bike. That's an original Harley-Davidson shift knob.

Left: Fabricator Kevin did this one for my Chop-Off bike. My sun logos are engraved lengthwise. The cool diamond knob is from Bling Cycles.

A good assortment of shift knobs, from antique to rare to car. There are so many options.

DISASSEMBLY

Again, this is the base for our custom-made ratchet-top levers, cut for us by Fabricator Kevin. They are available for sale as a core or as a whole lever through my website (www.chopperfreak.com) or eBay store.

Above: *The five-speed shifter, shown out of the bike for a much better view.*

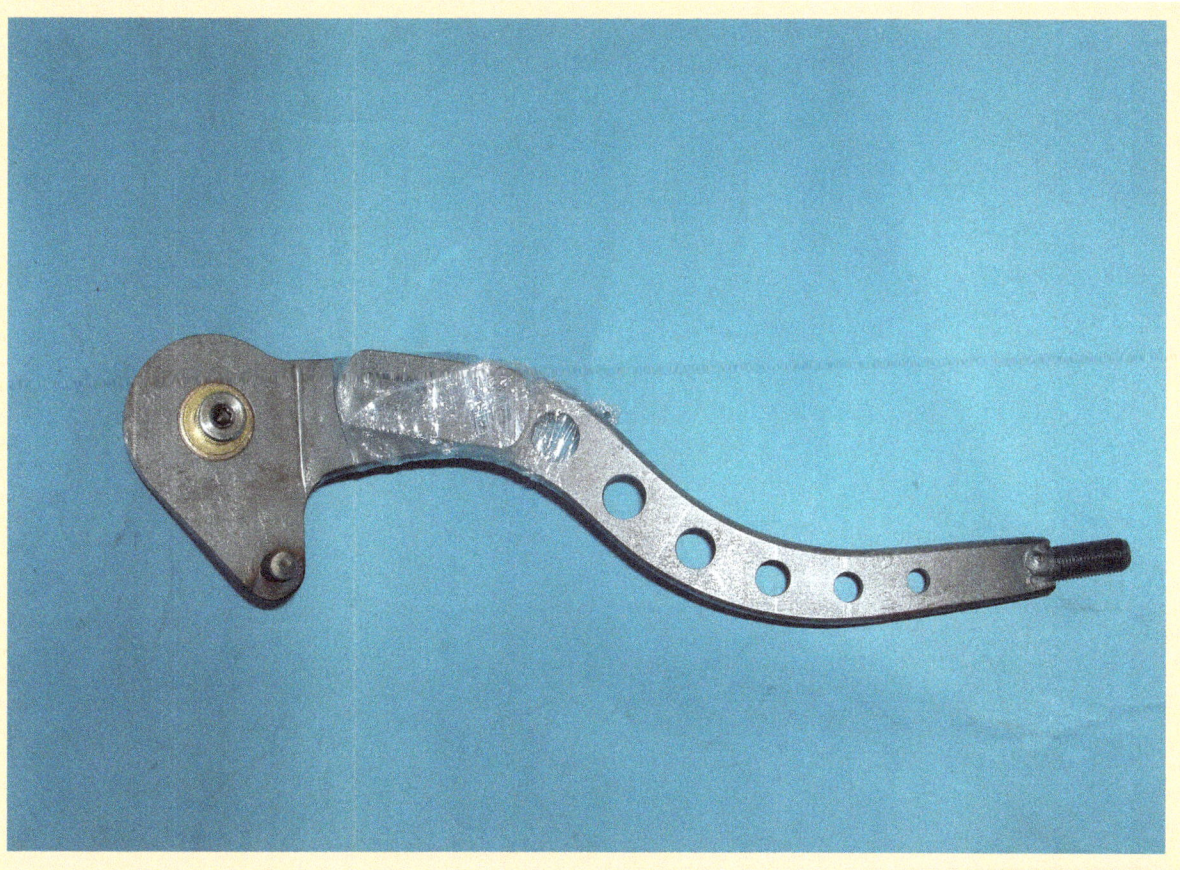

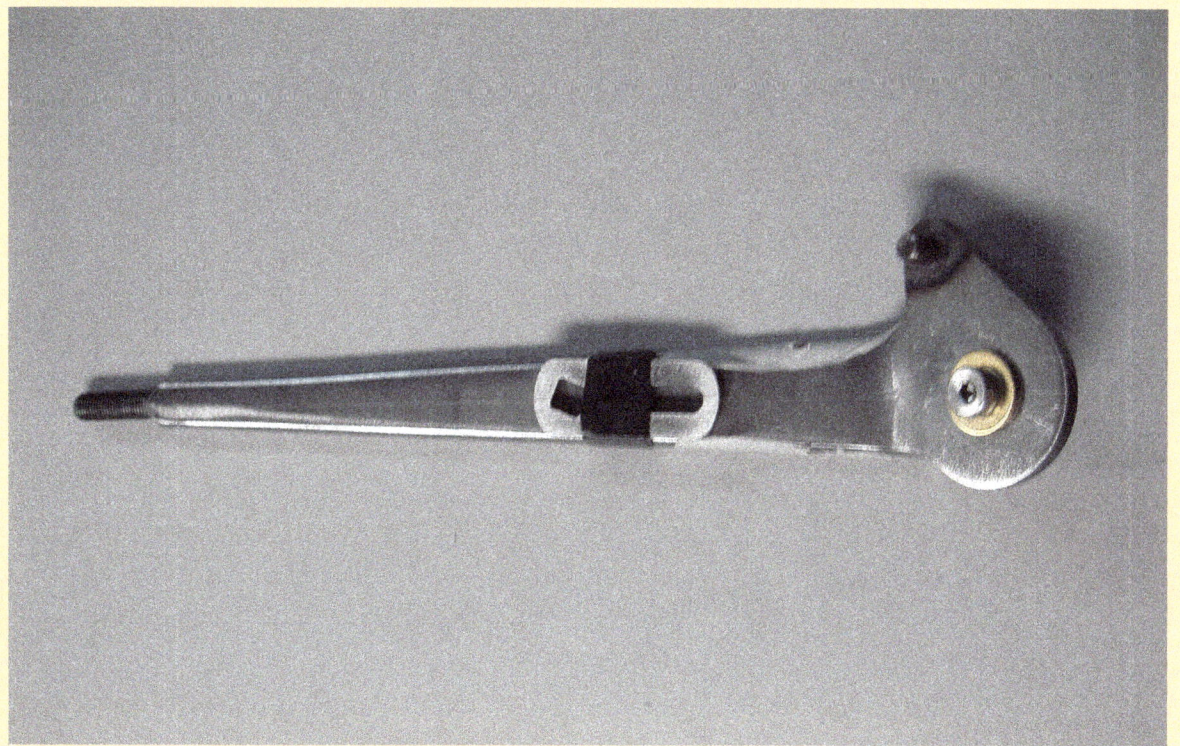

Two Fabricator Kevin kits for cow flop transmissions.

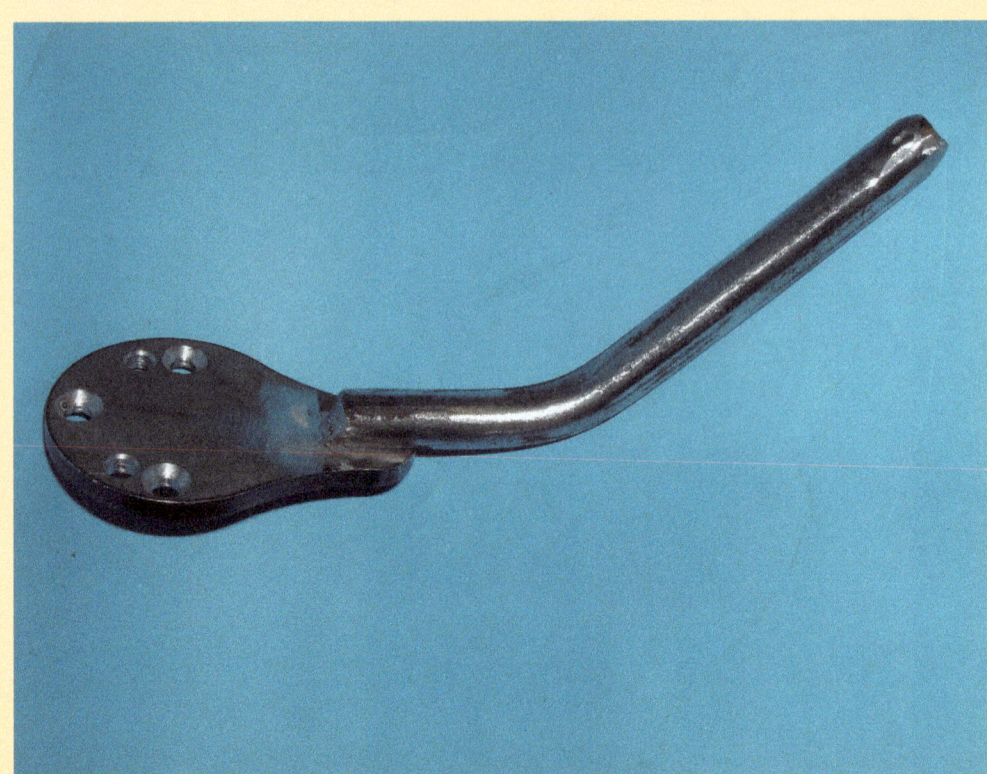

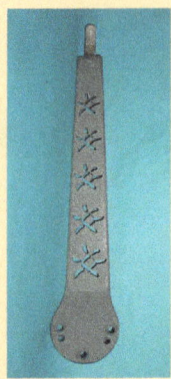

Above: *A better view of the sun logo shifter.*

Left: *Our custom shifter. This one is really short. Again, the best stuff can hardly be seen but is effective. I do any turns, any length, as needed.*

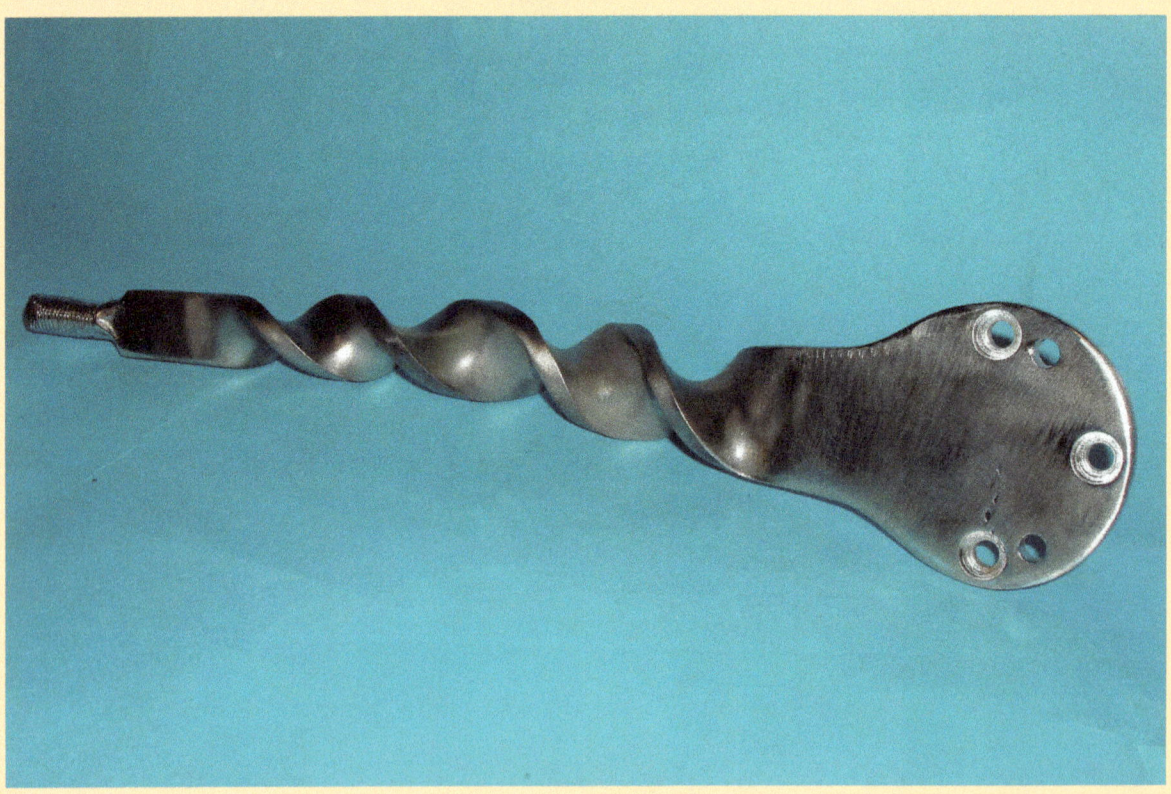

My twisted jockey lever in raw form, ready to ship to another customer or to go into one of my builds for the mockup. Chrome it, paint it, whatever.

Above: *I guess that says it all, made out of brass by our friend, Fabricator Kevin.*

Left: *I made this custom shifter a tank shift for one of Yuka's bikes. You can see the linkage and attachment. It's a spin-off on the old police shifters.*

Bicycle-pedal style. These were stock items in older bikes. They now come in several colors, and you can get brass inserts from Chica to make them even cooler (or you can make your own).

GASKETS

Since the motor is in pieces, install all new gaskets. There are a couple good tricks here to make them work better. We use glue (emblem adhesive or similar) and apply it to both sides of the gasket before placing. Make sure every single part of the surface is clean—no oil, dirt, etc. Some degreaser or brake cleaner will work great at getting the surface clean. There's also an old racing trick we used a lot on my race cars. Take a hole punch, and punch the surface where the gasket will be. Do it as many times as you please. This will leave an uneven surface for the gasket to adhere to. Those holes will bite the gasket and help in reducing any possible future leaks.

Don't be cheap. Replace all the gaskets, and remember the cork (or O-rings) on the pushrod tubes, too. And check your manual for the proper torque.

Make sure the gaskets and glue are not blocking any oil passages.

TIRES/WHEELS

I recommend new tires and new tubes on any new build. Of course, new wheel bearings are critical, as well.

Get these parts now while you have an opportunity to work on them. Stuff might be on back order, so when you are ordering and buying other parts, you might as well get these.

I use stainless-steel spokes in all my bikes. They are pretty simple to clean and last forever. Make sure you order the right spokes for your hub. I send my wheels to our friend Payo (our local Triumph and British bike guru) to spoke them and true them. I know how to do it, but what he charges is fair enough as long as I don't have to. Many of the Harley service manuals show how to work on your wheels, the pattern, etc. If you have a lot of spare time and patience, go ahead.

Assuming that you have your wheels back from painting, take them to a shop for mounting. Make sure the shop is careful or has a machine that won't scratch your fresh paint.

OTHER PARTS

This would also be the time to send the seat to the upholsterer or do it yourself. There are a lot of people out there who do very bitchin' jobs. I've had a couple bike seats done by Paul Cox, as well as Duane Ballard. Both are very, very good at what they do. But I have also upholstered seats myself for a mere $15, so it's your call. The shaping of the foam is as important, if not more, as the actual cover. If you must do it yourself, there are many resources available online, in books, and in magazines.

I could keep going about a million things that you might need to do while taking your bike apart. But the bottom line is that while taking your bike apart, you will also be working on sending parts out, finishing welds, getting new parts ordered, and keeping notes on work that needs to be done. You will optimize your time and effort now in order to minimize the time spent putting your bike together in the final assembly. Figure out what will be needed, what will you use, and remember that dreaded back orders will hold up your build and test your patience.

Nothing feels better than a build that flows. You can maximize your time, going step by step, while building the bike. Yes, it would be perfect to have everything you need right there at hand to keep the flow of the assembly. You can go back to the beginning of this book and notice that preparation is very important and probably one of the key jobs of this whole build. I make list after list of what I need, what needs to be done, and the steps I will take.

I also have a normal order of things in the way I work and the way parts will be used in the final assembly. I use Post-It notes and cardboard (a blackboard or dry erase board works very well, too) to keep track of what needs to be done at each step (assembly/mockup, disassembly, final assembly).

Again, everything goes at the speed of your free time and finances. So don't worry about when you start or if you don't have some part yet. All the previous pain or impatience will be forgotten when your final assembly starts to actually flow.

These pedals have been around for the longest time, and they are still cool. They come in metal or brass.

A friend sent me this pedal a long time ago, and it's the only one like it that I've seen, so I'm sure it's aftermarket. I know I will use it one of these days.

These are gold, but in white, the popsicle-style pedal is original Harley-Davidson stuff. It was also available in black or red. Black is the only one I've seen currently in production.

I made this brass kicker. It's not finished, but then again, it might be a good starting point for you to build your own.

DISASSEMBLY

Above and left: *We did not have much space for the battery, so we came up with this battery base, which also holds the voltage regulator and serves as an anchor point for the rear fender. It's another multiuse item that blends in with the overall flow of the bike. We measured for the battery size and welded the cage together with metal straps. The bung welded into it is the fender anchor, and the two recessed holes on the bottom attach our voltage regulator bracket. In this case, we welded the cage to the frame. If you see Canito's 1974 XL up close, you can see the finished product.*

When I built the Chop-Off bike, it seemed that the neck area had too much metal, but I do need the reinforcement—jumping road ramps while doing 70 miles per hour and popping wheelies stresses the frame. While there was way too much purple in that area, I decided to keep the brass touches and add some plates. Ñeco, who is a local artisan, engraved the plates by hand and added some question marks and rivets for effect. Then I bolted them to the neck plates. It was a simple and inexpensive solution.

I did the templates in cardboard and then used a thin sheet of brass to cut the proper form. Here you see them ready to be engraved.

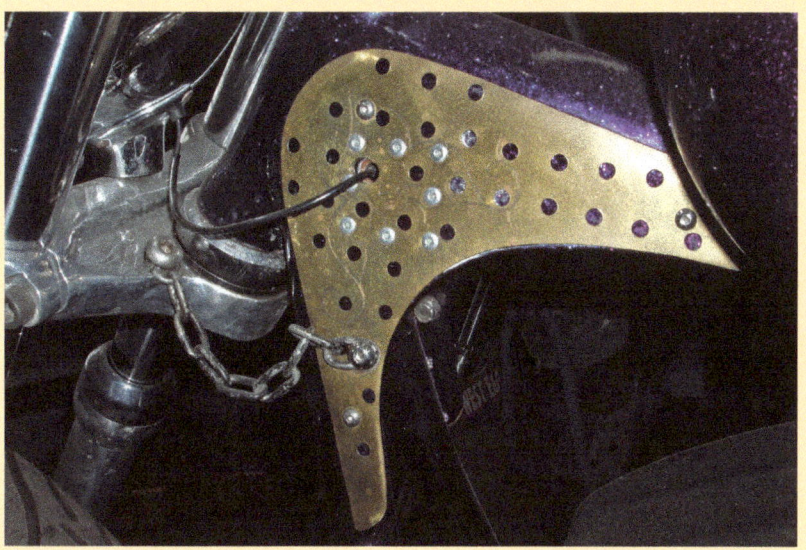

Here is the finished product, engraved and installed. I drilled a hole to slip the headlight wires through, and it's attached by screws and very easy to take off if needed. It did bring the contrast I wanted. Sure, this is not something necessary, but it added to the bike, and the devil is in the details.

CHAPTER 7
PAINT

Sometimes the hardest part of a build is choosing a color and scheme for your bike. I prefer things to be as simple as possible. On my bikes, kandy colors and metalflake are the norm, with occasional simple graphics, panels, teardrops, scallops, and derivations of such. Pinstriping by itself looks really cool, as well. I rarely use flames, but alas, they always look cool and never go out of style. I tend to lean more toward flames on choppers and almost never on a bobber.

There are many books available (including several by JoAnn Bortles, published by Motorbooks) that can help you immensely in this area. They will provide you with ideas, hints, tips, techniques, and a bunch more useful information for your paint job. Like always, the more research you do, the more you learn, and the better off you are at the end.

Some home builders will use the rattle-can method, usually flat black. But even with that, there's always a lot of prep work involved. Just because you are using a $2.98 can of spray paint doesn't mean the bike has to look like a $2.98 paint job. It all depends on how carefully you handle the most important step of the painting process: the preparation.

PREP

As was shown before, as soon as we receive the frame, or any other bare metal part, we clean it up using water and soap, sand it, and then bomb spray it. (What I call bomb spray is simply using spray paint from a rattle can as a base primer.) We live in the Caribbean, and being on an island means you are surrounded by salt water with a very high concentration of corrosive mist in the air (as with any place close to the sea or in high humidity). Plus, all the natural oils from hands and touching accelerate the rusting of the bare metal. The build will take some time, so we must keep that rust off our project. Trust me—there will be lot less work involved later on. Rust and dirt are the worst enemies of a good finish and end product.

We bring the frame to the table already bombed up. When there's a need to weld, we just grind the area's surface for much better penetration as needed and simply repaint when we're done. Make sure the welds are ground nice and smooth before painting them over.

Take your sweet time doing this. Just because it's an inexpensive build does not mean it has to look cheap. I really

A couple of examples of our rattle-can primed frames. In the first photo, we actually used primer. I had to add it to the book since it's one of those rare cases.

Pepo is helping us out by spraying this one with a rattle can.

Green and whatever else was left—it kind of looks like a military bike, or maybe a frog on acid.

Even if you are still planning on bomb spraying as your final coating, you'll want to mold the frame. We also take time to fill and mold the gas tank and fender smooth. Remember, prepping correctly is a must since it will show through all the way to the final step of your paint job. After all the molding and smoothing is finished, we spray the frame with high-quality primer. Again, we don't want that rust from inside the tubing to break through to our job. You'll want to use a high-quality primer, especially around the gas tank, where fuel fumes can create bubbles in your gas tank's finish (and that nasty-looking bubbling around the gas cap).

When all this work is done, making the decision between spraying with good paint and clearcoat or a couple coats of bomb spray should be calculated wisely. Since we are building an inexpensive bike, it won't make or break the bank to get a nice paint job. But the small investment will pay for itself in quality, duration, luster, and protection . . . well worth it, since it's also expensive and time-consuming to take the bike apart and re-apply a cheap paint job gone sour.

Even when we do use flat black, we use black mixed with a flattening agent rather than spray-can stuff. Go wild and try out the same method with any other color. We have been experimenting with other colors flattened out, and they do look different and funky. I still lean toward deep, rich kandies, but that's my preference.

Paint is not limited to the frame and sheet metal. We paint wheels, hubs, sliders, and whatever parts we feel are in need of a spray. Once again, we're always considering the smoothness and flow of the whole build. There are other options, obvious ones like chrome and powdercoating, but I still prefer paint for a couple very solid reasons. Paint is easy and quick to apply, durable, can be retouched, and it's less expensive with a much faster turnaround.

We are trying to put together an inexpensive bike, so chrome will blow up our budget. Powdercoating is not cheap either and takes some time. But paint, more so in areas that are easily chipped, ends up being a much smarter choice. The same person who is painting your build will spray other smaller items, I'm sure. Or, if you are doing it yourself, it will be just a little more work and lot less money spent.

There are other alternative finishes, including polishing and engine turning and such, but please don't go crazy. I don't think a whole engine-turned bike looks cool, and neither does a polished bike from front to rear. But I really do like a mixture of polished and painted parts on my bikes (besides the frame and sheet metal), and I guess it shows. Go ahead and dare to paint stuff that is not normally painted. It's also a very good way to bring life to a certain area that might look boring with the same finish as everything else. There may be some parts that have chipped, scratched, or pitted, and with a fresh coat of paint they will look like new or even better than new. Better yet, it might look different, which happens to be one of our goals: to be different from everyone else.

prefer the way smooth frames look. Clean is the proper word. Don't cheat on this part of the process. Take the time to really smooth out all those welds, joints, and maybe even the tubes themselves. Good builders can tell if the extra mile has been taken, and we do notice those tiny details that others miss.

CHOOSING A COLOR

Choosing a color (or colors) is often a pain. For many, it's the hardest part of the whole build. I guess it's the inability to decide among so many cool available colors and the fact that, for the most part, your expense will be a decision you will live with for a long time.

I always start with color charts. You can get these from all the major paint manufacturers and most shops. I tend to lean toward the weird colors, but for the most part we've tested and examined them and know what we'll end up with. If we don't, it can be an expensive fix. Right now, our next batch of bikes ranges from gunmetal gray to kandy metalflaked brown. There are 11 bikes in the works, so we've got the chore of choosing paint that will not repeat itself. Then again, you can never go wrong with black.

I won't spend too much time on techniques and such, since most home builders will leave the painting up to the experts. We use House of Kolor paint almost exclusively. Their method of using tints and base colors will largely reduce the amount of paint you have to buy (in case you plan on painting more bikes at a further date). Their system is imitated by other companies now and simply uses added hues and materials to change tint and effects. It also seems like their colors last longer and have a resistance to fading and such. We are freaky about their metalflake and have been for a long time. Large chunks of metalflake look extremely bitchin' on any cool, older bike. One of the standout painters for this older style is a guy who calls himself "The Harpoon." I still don't know how he achieves such cool metalflake jobs.

House of Kolor and metalflake, the bread and butter of our builds.

Left and below: *Black with burnt orange stripes (Canito's 1974 Sportster).*

CHOOSING A PAINTER

If you are doing it yourself, then choosing your painter is obvious. But most of us can't paint, so start asking friends or your local body shop. Depending on the paint job, there's no need for a motorcycle-specific painter. A reliable body or paint shop can do the job. Or, if you're doing designs and custom graphics on the gas tank and fender, you can find someone who does it for a living (and you might save $$ since the hard work is done already).

Pepo, my local guy, paints all of our bikes. He is a friend and customer, and I have built him a couple bikes. He owns a body shop, so we've always had total access to start experimenting with our bikes and getting his guys better at painting them. He paints fairly quick and at a good price. Better yet, when I've been in a super hurry, he has not failed once to accommodate me. It would be cool if everyone could work like this with their painter, although I know it's not always possible. That is part of why you should shop around, ask friends, etc.

continued on page 128

The Chop-Off/Indian Larry tribute bike. Pinstripe on gas cap by Caffeine—check the ghosted question marks and my sun logo.

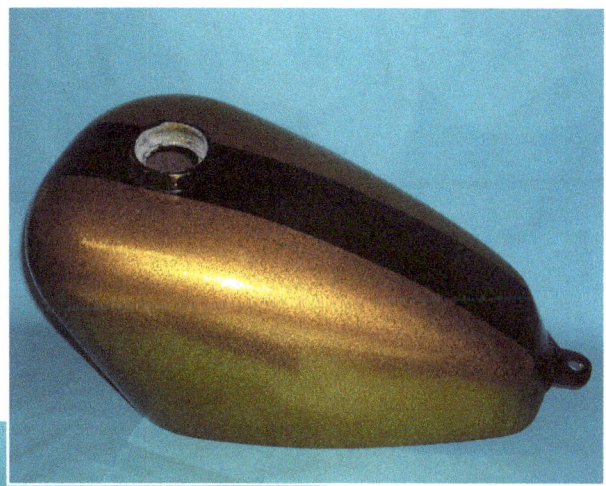

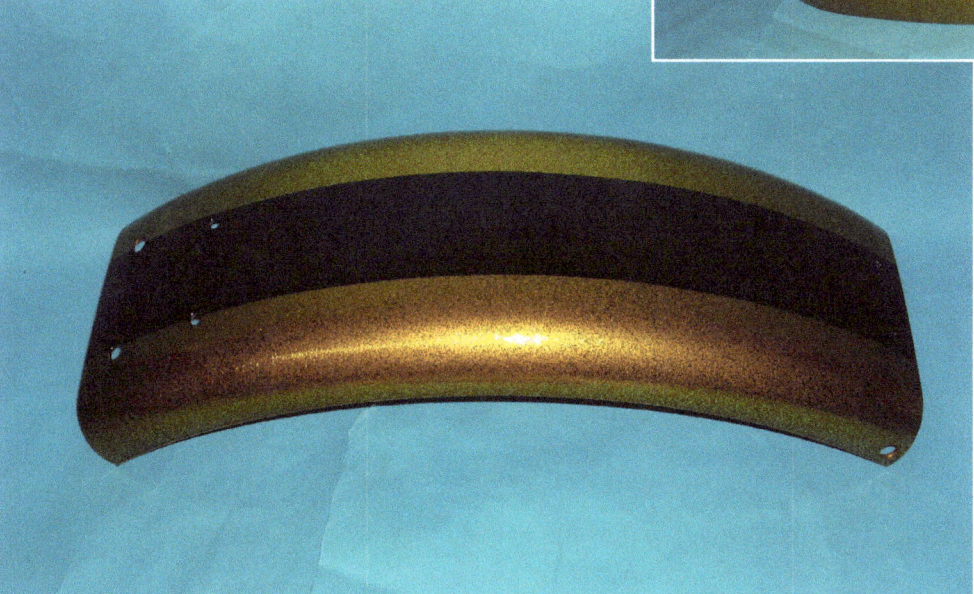

Above and left: Antonio's 1950 build—pagan gold and black stripe. You'll notice our paint jobs are as simple as the bikes themselves.

A Sportster rigid chopper frame, ready to start final assembly.

Tangerine orange frame.

PAINT

Left and below: *The Journey Museum bobber. Scallops are cool, and they will never go out of style. Even the pinstripe is metalflaked.*

PAINT

The barrel oil tank, hand-striped graphics by Unkle D.

continued from page 125

Stay away from those big-buck paint jobs. It will just blow the whole budget and the bike you are building will look much better with a simple paint job, not looking like an Easter egg hunt.

Choose wisely. There's nothing worse than having your bike at a paint shop forever. Been there, trust me. I swear, one of my past painters knew every excuse in the book as to why he couldn't paint my bike today. I remember a bike I took to him when his wife was pregnant, and I swear the little bastard was already talking by the time I could pick it up. Needless to say, it was a total waste of time and money. By then, I wanted to change the whole bike anyway; I never did use the paint job.

On the other hand, don't use a painter just because he's fast. If the paint job is crappy, you also lost time and money. Again, look around and choose wisely. Your pocket and heart will thank you.

Lali's tangerine fender.

Pichigui's 1973 cobalt blue gas tank by Pepo Paints.

CHOOSING PAINT

We use House of Kolor from Valspar and have been using it for quite a long time. But there are a couple companies working on (and already selling) similar products, such as SEM and PPG. Both are great paints. Actually, my 1962 Impala SS is being painted with PPG as I write this, and it's looking very good. We have also done a few bikes with SEM and had very good results. Still, I have to give every new paint product time to see how it holds up. Like I said before, the durability of House of Kolor is tops in my book.

Need to save money? Well, there are similar brands that can be used as a base color and might save you a couple Washingtons. Or, instead of kandy, just paint your bike a solid color. That should lower the bill considerably. Again, ask around. Some shops have paint companies they swear by and get good deals from them. So, as with anything in your build, homework is key.

A good paint job makes or breaks a bike. It's not everything, but it does add a lot to the whole project. And a fresh, shiny paint job makes everything look much better.

CHOOSING A DESIGN

Your design needs special attention. A simple bike with an outrageous paint job does not look good. Simplicity is important, and I do not give the choice to my customers of choosing a design with custom graphics simply because (and this may be pompous of me) I believe I can choose a paint scheme to follow the flow of the bike. While wolves, Indians, skulls, and such might be cool to some (and might look badass on certain bikes), I really follow my simplicity rule all the way through, so our designs are very simple, as well. Some scallops, a teardrop, maybe some ghosted designs (ghosting is when you can barely see the designs at plain sight, but when the light hits it right they do come to life), maybe a simple racing stripe or line, some pinstriping, or an emblem from an older bike, and that's it. In one of our bikes (Wicho's 1952 Pan, to be exact), we just added a couple Hot Wheels stickers (since the paint was going to be temporary) and everyone got to know the bike as the Hot Wheels bike. They looked pretty cool, and still today people ask about the Hot Wheels Panhead, although it's been changed for quite some time.

Flat black... once in a while, we do use it. It's actually gloss black with flattening agent.

I do not like busy paint jobs, and I certainly do not like theme bikes either. There are so many simple things that you can do to your bike that, although not original, will certainly be unique. A few days ago, I saw a bike with a couple Sailor Jerry designs on it. To me, it looked cool and simple as it can be.

I am not a total dictator when it comes to paint. I do work with the customers for certain things. A long time ago, a customer wanted a paint job that would remind him of his kids. Of course, I refused to splatter their faces all over the place, so I came up with the idea of having their hand prints on the bike. The kids had a ball getting dirty, their tiny painted hands all over the bike, and the bike ended up looking kinda cool. But more important, it was different and personal. I recently built a bob/chop for one of my customers from Ireland. I decided to paint it kandy green with ghosted clovers all over the metal, in addition to a couple racing stripes. He does not know and does not expect it, but I think it's a cool addition. I don't do flags or country-themed bikes, but if you can figure out subtle ways to show people where you're from, it's a classier look.

One more thing: the more complex and detailed the paint scheme, the harder and more expensive it will be to repair. And since these bikes are meant to be ridden hard, and they will be, paint chipping will happen. If you want to do something with your favorite beer in mind, a logo here or there is cool, but a rolling billboard is not. I can't repeat it enough.

Always keep in mind that simple designs are way cooler than overblown, complex, multicolored paint jobs. An overdone design scheme can come off like wearing a penguin suit (aka tuxedo) to the beach. The paint scheme should fit and flow with the bike.

TECHNIQUES

This is just a very short explanation of the different design styles that are widely used on bikes. For more details and information, you should refer to JoAnn Bortles' books or any specific book for this technique.

Airbrush

The art of painting with a small air gun, blowing air and paint at the same time, can produce anything from very simple designs to supercomplicated murals. I've seen airbrush artists who will put to shame any of the higher-arts dudes.

If you are trying it yourself, remember that the paint used for a T-shirt is not the same as the one for your bike. Practice on spare parts and scrap metal first, and have fun with it. Who knows? You might have a hidden talent.

Stencils

There's a lot of stencil use going on these days, and with computers and plotters it's easy to achieve what seemed impossible a few years ago. Those very tiny, intricate designs are now possible thanks to our friend, the PC.

We paint most of our wheels. It lasts longer, and you can retouch in case of chipping.

Freehand

I've seen many people work freehand (taping the design), for example, on flames that I swear are much better than anything a perfect computer can do. Just to drop a couple names, Arlen Ness and Dave Perewitz . . . if anyone were in the Flames Hall of Fame (if such thing existed), it'd be these two guys for sure.

There are also various techniques for achieving freehand designs. Some people use chalk, then tape, or rice paper (cutting designs like a dress pattern), pencils, etc. Of course, the freehand part refers to a human doing all the prep and taping, not machines.

Pinstriping

Pinstriping seemed to be a lost art, but thanks to the renaissance of the old school (rat rods, bobbers, choppers, etc.), it is catching up again. Guys and gals are picking up the long brushes and sign paint once more and giving it a try. The designs can be as simple as a few lines or super-intricate symmetrical forms. One thing is for sure, they are always cool. Then again, I am partial to the older way of doing things.

What's even cooler about striping is that it can be done after you have your bike painted and assembled. So if you do not have the coin now, it can always be added later.

Faux Textures

I bet you have seen faux-textured bikes in magazines or on TV. Rust, polished metal, brushed metal, copper or brass, or other fabricated textures—there's so much going on, a trip to the art shop or prop shop (if you live in Cali) can be a treasure hunt.

Here's where coming up with an idea and working with it can achieve pretty cool stuff. Give a workout to your brain. There are also paints that give you a certain finish, like marbles and chameleons. There are some flakes that, when painted over black, give you pretty cool results.

Right now, I am experimenting with different techniques on metal. Mixtures of household items will give certain colors and tones to bare metal. I am in the research step still, but pretty soon I'll start trying them out on actual builds. Have you seen what your wife does to walls and such, with sponges, Brillo pads, anything and everything? Try them out. Who knows? You might end up with a super unique and cool bike.

TIPS TO KEEP IN MIND

Your paint job and design scheme should go and flow with your build.

Choose wisely who will paint your bike, and try to have the best-quality paint job you can afford.

A good paint ain't cheap, and a cheap paint ain't good.

You can never go wrong with gloss black. It will always look cool, and the bike will look clean.

There's a lot more to all of this, and as I said before, I am just passing briskly over it since there are many books about paint out there. I am a sucker for research and learning new stuff. I do not paint, but I know techniques, what goes with what, mixtures, results, etc., and that's a super plus when talking to my painter or customers.

Last but not least, painting your bike is one of the most important details for your finished product. You can have the trickest bike in the world, but if the paint sucks, the whole thing sucks. Everything needs to complement accordingly.

We use the Beugler pinstriping tool a lot. I wish I could pinstripe with brushes, but for simple jobs, this is a savior.

These cool parts are old, they have appeal, and they are hard to get. If you have them, lucky you. If you see them around cheap, buy them or give me a call.

Paughco is still making these transmission kicker covers, and they are still cool.

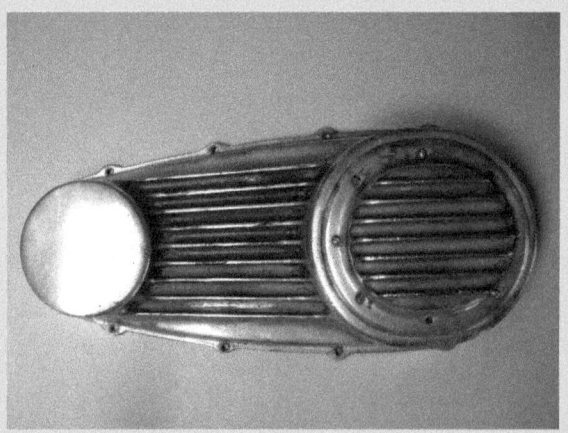

An outer primary from Imperial. These were very popular 30 years ago.

As you can see, I'm using real Imperial parts. No fakes, no repros.

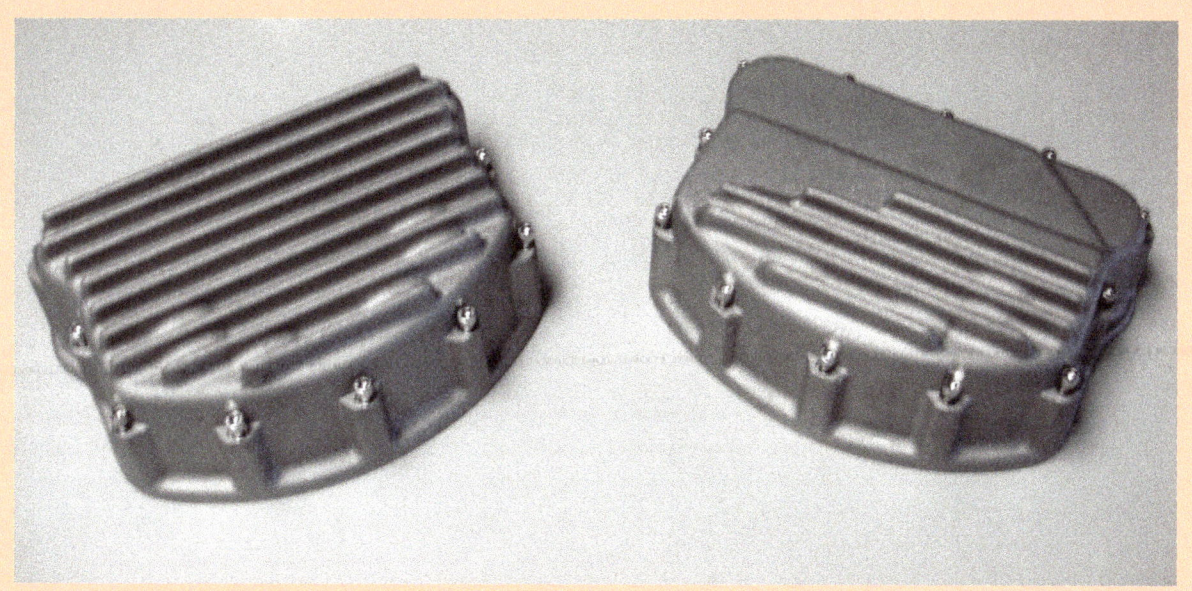

Here is a shot of the front and rear Panhead covers from Custom Cycle Engineering. I just love these parts.

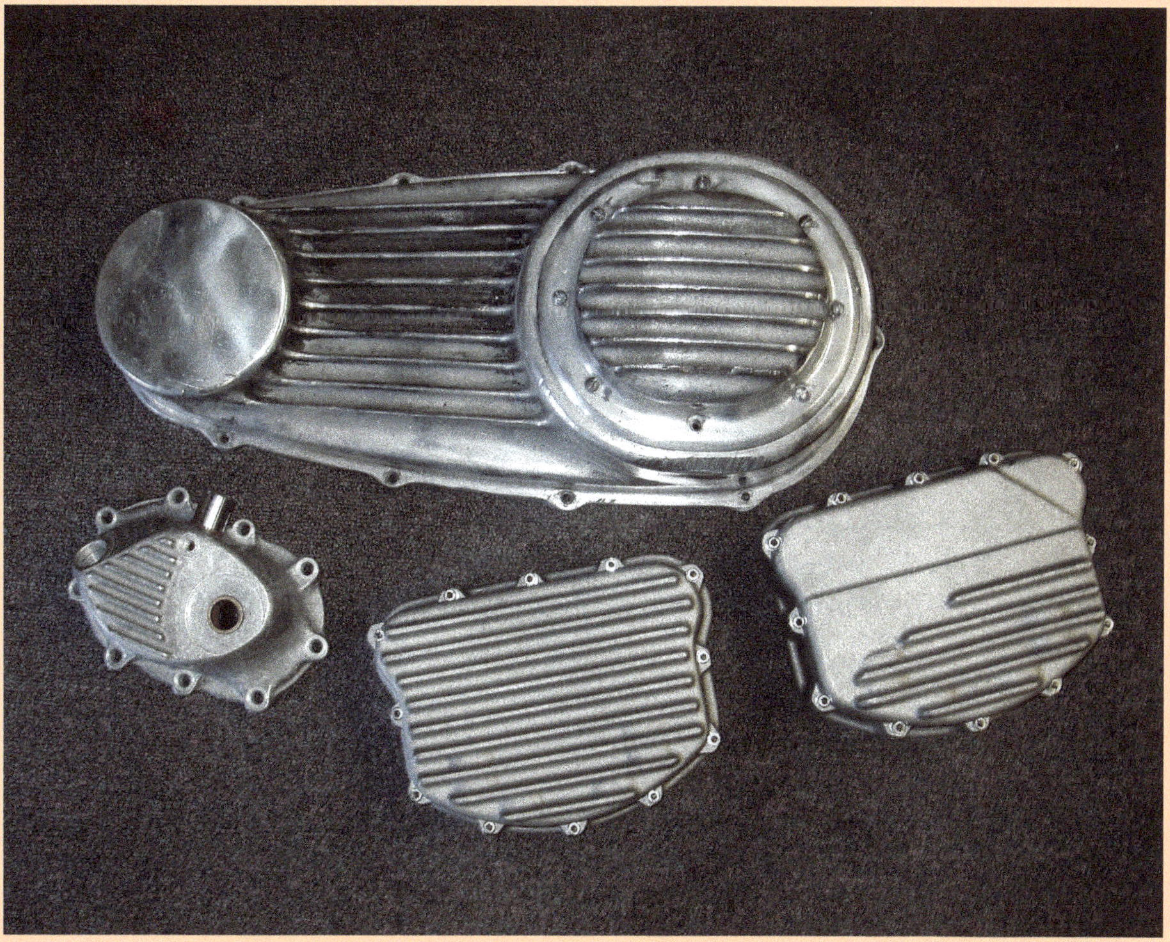

A shot of everything together, right before sending the parts to Bradley the Polisher to do his magic. You may notice on the Journey Museum bike that these parts are smooth and shiny, and they look like gold.

CHAPTER 8
FINAL ASSEMBLY

I guess all good things must come to an end, although this is the very good end. This is the step where you will see your hard work, money, and ideas become something tangible and something that you will enjoy for quite some time. But even better, it will be something that you created—your baby.

To some, this part goes super fast, and for others, it seems to be in extreme slow motion. Things that we forgot (bolts, parts, etc.) will get on our nerves now. Stopping the frantic completion to go fetch some stupid bolts will try our patience. Then again, your job is almost done! So enjoy the whole thing. Soon, very soon, you will be riding your bike.

LET'S GET STARTED

Let's say you are drooling over your freshly painted frame and sheet metal right now. Everything that needs to be done to the motor, transmission, front end, etc., is already done, and you have most of what you need. So, if you already have everything you need to start the assembly, where do you start?

First, clean up the area where the build will take place. If you have a lift, load the frame on it and set it where you feel most comfortable. Sometimes I prefer a lower, even surface. I have several 4x4 boards that keep the frame level and safe. Once these are in place, I cover them with an old sheet or blanket in order to avoid scratching the bottom tubes of the freshly painted frame. (If the paint is really fresh, you should wait until it cures. Your painter can tell you how long.)

I strongly advise you to be very, very careful during the entire final assembly. Remember that the frame and sheet metal are painted now, and with all the metal parts and tools flying around, chips and scratches come easily, and they'll ruin your final product.

Urethane paint will chip and crack when you bolt parts tightly against it. So any surface where there will be pressure or bolts tightened, etc., need to be shaved off. By that, I mean get a few good razor blades and peel your new paint job where it's needed. I know it sounds crazy, but this will

We get a razor blade and an X-ACTO knife and start cutting paint away. Here, you can see the transmission plate mounts.

It should kinda look like this. We cut all the edges first, so that just in case there's a mistake, we don't rip off the cool House of Kolor kandy.

We cut a template of the motor mount and mark accordingly. It's easier and much safer than putting the engine on and then taking it off.

FINAL ASSEMBLY

After it's been cut off, we also trim the edges so the paint won't run off.

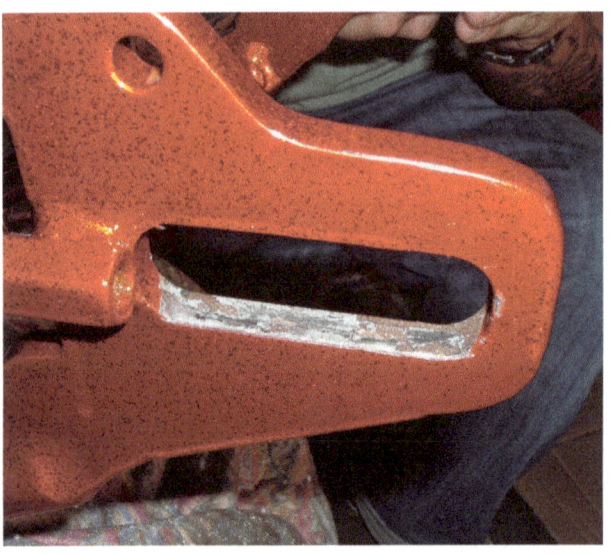

Since all we do are rigids, we cut off the inner axle plate where the axle will slide freely. Trim all the edges. An X-ACTO knife is much better for this project.

save your paint later on. The motor mounts (top and bottom) are a must, so let's start with them.

You should cut along the sharp edges with the blade. Doing so prevents the paint crack from running, and where you cut is where it stops. Some people make a cutout of the motor mount shape (front and rear). If you do so, I suggest allowing some space between the actual paint and motor. In other words, over cut. If you are fussy, you can blade off the paint or simply take a pneumatic angle grinder and sand the paint off. The top motor mount should receive a similar shave. If you are using good washers, then only shave the inside of the loop so the bolt won't peel the paint off.

Other important pressure areas are the axle plates, so the axle movement and adjustment won't scrape off the paint. Speaking of which, go through the whole bike with tap on hand and clean every single threaded area. The bolt holes that are not threaded should be cleaned with a drill and bit. Remember that paint adds a good layer to every surface, and even though it's minimal, it's still a layer that can set your fitting off a bit.

We get the trusty drill and a sharp bit to clean every hole that has already been made. In bungs that will have direct contact with metal, we also shave off the paint and trim the edges.

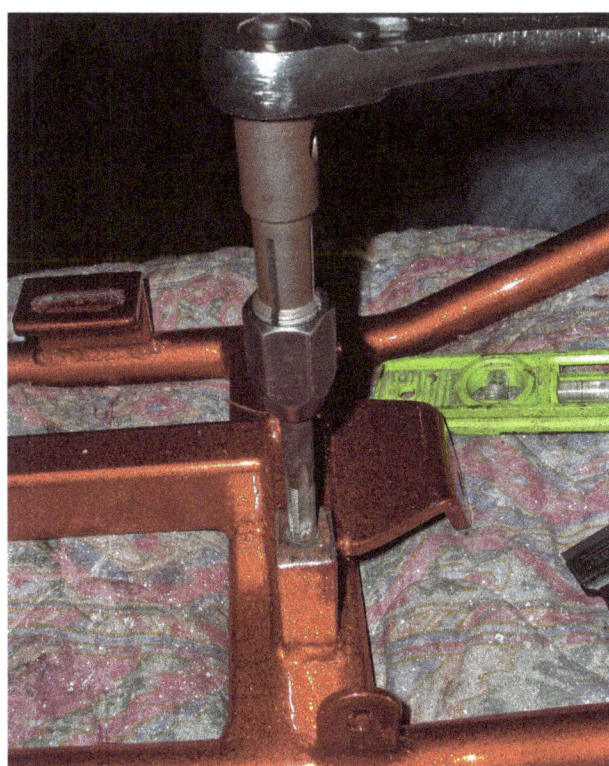

Every single thread on the bike will get cleaned with a tap set. Paint sneaks all over the place, so clean it up well. We also cut the edges with a razor blade. Note: When I say cut the edges, I mean that we cut across sections to stop the paint in case it happens to peel for whatever reason. In some parts, the cut is invisible. In others, it's so fine that it does not make much of a difference.

It will take some time, but you will have to look for every single area on your bike where something will be attached and clean/shave off the paint.

Once you are totally certain that everything is clean (and you should do this before installing any parts), then it's finally time to start bolting on parts. Or maybe not. Be sure to tape everything off that might get scratched while working on the assembly (blue painter's tape is great since it's less sticky than masking tape and won't rip the paint).

ENGINE AND TRANSMISSION

As on the mockup, let's start with placing the engine in its proper location. The engine can really scratch up the paint, so be very, very careful. Have a couple friends around for help (and they do need to help, not crack jokes and drink beer while you sweat your new metalflake paint job, holding a 100-plus-pound motor). If you are sitting on the bike looking forward (and let's think like this from now on), the engine will only go in from your right to left. The oil pump is on the right side and will be sticking out. Also remember to leave off the carburetor, motor mount, and anything else that might make life more difficult, scratch the paint, or stop the installation.

Your friends can help by guiding the motor without sliding, jerking, or shaking it. In other words, no matter how difficult and heavy it is, the motor should go in smoothly. Once the motor is in, you can slide the bolts in place and screw in the nuts. Do not tighten them now. You're just trying the keep the engine in place (and make sure all your nuts and bolts are accounted for).

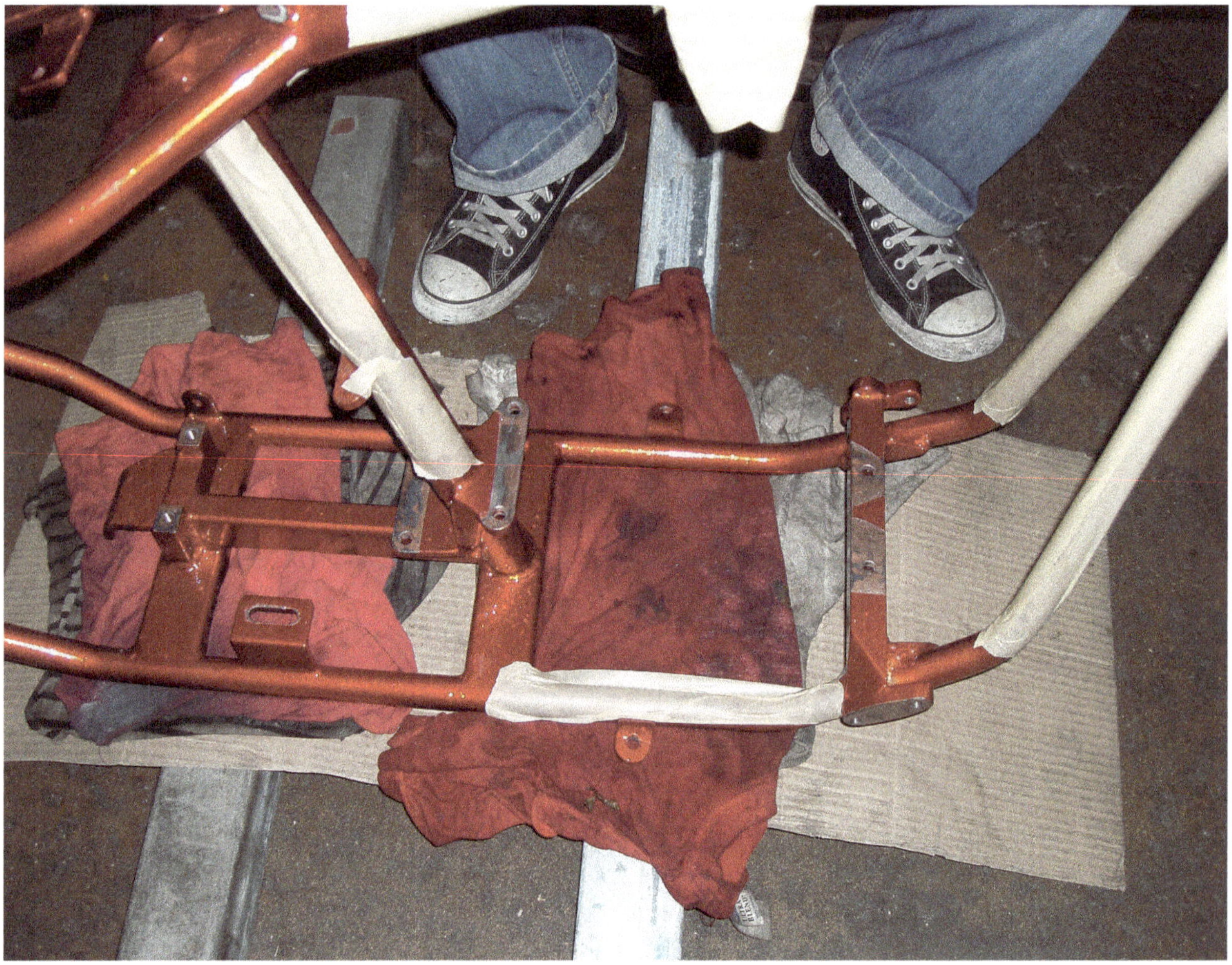

As you can see, the motor mounts have been cleaned up. I prefer blue tape, but masking is what we had, so we taped certain areas to try to avoid scratches. We placed the frame on the ground atop two 4x4s covered with old rags (the same would be done on the lift).

More taping and shots from different angles. The frame is super stable on top of the two 4x4s.

Left: *The motor is in, with no scratches and no mishaps. So now that the engine is in, let's go to the transmission. Remember, we follow these steps in order to keep the bike/frame balanced.*

Below: *Since we've already peeled the transmission mount, we place the painted transmission plate in place (and make sure we cut it right).*

FINAL ASSEMBLY

A view of the motor and transmission plate; the tape will be ripped off soon.

FINAL ASSEMBLY

The transmission plate is bolted, slathered with Loctite, and tightened.

Slide transmission installed from right to left. Make sure you don't hit anything or chip the paint.

Next comes the transmission. Bolt in the transmission plate, and very carefully place the transmission. I prefer to slide the tranny in from left to right while holding the kicker arm. Once it's in place, screw in the nuts but do not tighten them. (Remember to add Loctite to anything and everything you tighten for good. I tend to write down what needs to be tightened so I don't forget later. It's a good idea to double-check them all.)

FRONT END

Once our build is balanced by the engine and tranny, I work on the front end making sure that all the paint has been off the neck and there's no residue on the bearing races. While making sure that the neck bearings are packed, go ahead and install the triple trees. Again, do not tighten them fully until the fork tubes are into place. Make sure the pinch bolts are tight, the tubes have fork oil in them, and everything is OK; then tighten the top tree bolt (check the appropriate service manual for torque specs).

If you have the bike on a lift, this is the perfect time to also put on the front wheel. Make sure the bearings are new and packed, and grease the front axle. You might need some help if the bike is too low on the ground. Once this is done, secure the front wheel to the lift's vise.

I'm sure there will be a temptation at this point to bolt on as many parts as possible. Well, go ahead if you want to . . . this is the time. Get that headlight, those risers and bars, install the bushings (I highly recommend urethane handlebar bushings), and don't forget to add Loctite to all the bolts.

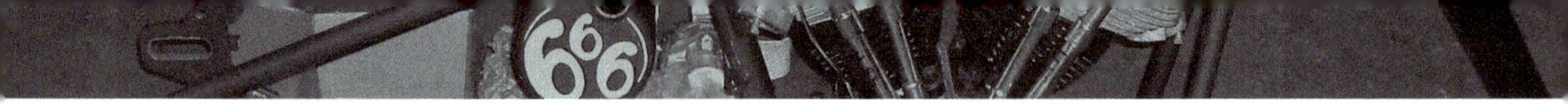

After packing the bearings and greasing the tree axle, we place the bottom tree. There are different ways to mount different triple trees; see the mockup part for another example. The older FL-style trees require a nut before the top triple tree. We place it loosely to check if everything fits. Don't forget Loctite. Check your manual for specific torque on your triple tree.

The top clamp is in place, loosely, in order to check that everything is OK.

A top view. We add the lock tab and nut with Loctite. We then check that everything is looking good and go for the sliders.

We slide the tubes, making sure that the pinch bolts are loose. Add a bit of assembly lube to make your job easier and prevent scratches on the tubes; also check the trees for any marks, and sand if needed.

With everything in place, make sure the sliders went all the way up on the trees. Tighten the pinch bolts, and recheck the top nut with the added weight. Now we are ready to keep on building.

FINAL ASSEMBLY

OIL TANK AND REAR END

In order to have the rear tire in place, you might need to do a couple things first. Loosely place the oil tank in position (depending on the way you mounted it, check if you can reach the bolts and nuts for tightening). The rear fender should go in place as well and be tightened with struts and all. If you have a fender-mounted stop light, this will be the right moment to install it, as well. Remember to route the taillight wiring in a way that will not rub the tire. After all this is done, place the rear tire, brake caliper, and other components in that area before sliding the rear axle into place. (Remember to check the bearings and grease the axle.)

Now you should have a level bike to work with. Check if the axle slides back and forth freely. If it does not, go back and shave off any paint that might have been left. Also check the spacers and where they make contact with the axle plates; I recommend shaving that paint area, too. Finally, check that none of the bolts or nuts rub the tire and, of course, that it spins freely and easy.

Going back to the oil tank, check the routing of the lines, and also make sure that your fittings are there and in the right direction. If you happen to have any electrical components hidden in the oil tank, make sure that all the proper holes are there. It's easier to work on the oil tank while not on the bike, of course, but if everything seems fine, go ahead and tighten it. Double-check the clearance of the jockey lever, coil, or anything else that might be in the area. Also, double-check other components and the routing of the oil lines.

Here's a shot of our painted barrel oil tank, ready to mount. Needless to say, this is the fun part of the whole build.

I prefer and recommend rubber oil lines. They are flexible, inexpensive, and easier to hide (plus they work very well). Most copper lines are not the right diameter, and steel braid will eat away at anything it rubs against. Since the idea here is keeping stuff out of sight and saving bucks, rubber oil lines are the simpler solution.

We are starting to see progress, and it's starting to look like a bike. Treat yourself and loosely place any other parts you have, such as the gas tank, seat, etc. This will give you an idea of what you have and what it will look like. Remember that this is just an idea step. Most of these items will come back off when you do the electrical stuff, so take a good look (and a few photos). Only you will know if it's looking like what you had in mind.

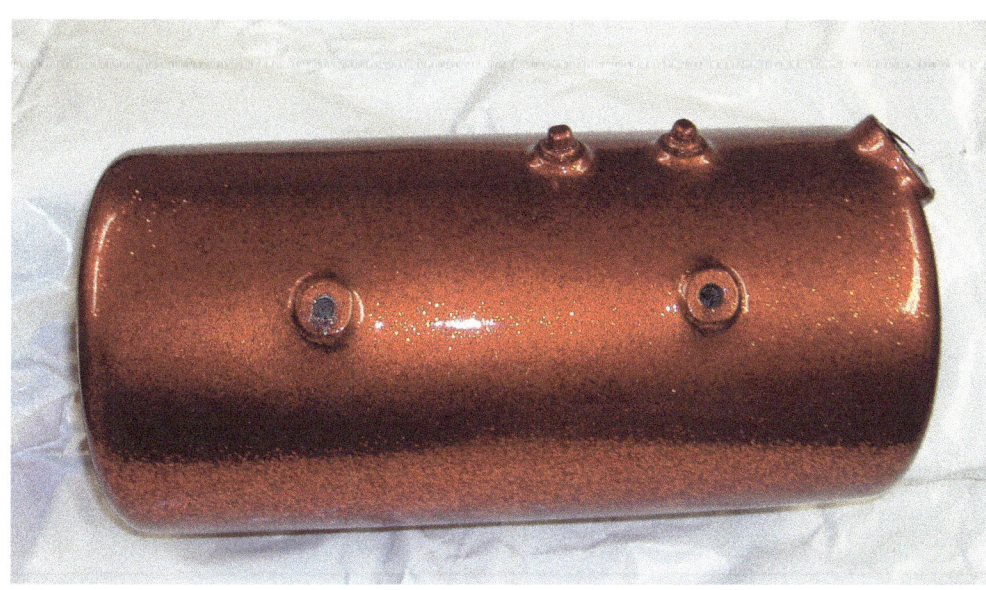

Another angle of the painted tank. Notice that we tapped the threads, and the fitting threads have been covered in order to avoid getting any paint or particles inside.

The oil tank is in place with bolts tight (remember Loctite). So far, everything is working as planned, so that is cool.

FINAL ASSEMBLY

Side shot of the oil tank, transmission, and engine in place. Now this is looking like something.

MOTOR MOUNTS AND PRIMARY

This might be a good time to tighten the motor mounts, top and bottom. The oldest trick in the book is tightening the rear mount first and then checking for any gap clearance in the front. If there's any clearance, fill the gap with shims (a soda or beer can). Tighten the top motor mount at the motor. If there's any gap on the frame top mount, add washers. (If you fabricated the motor mount, there should not be any space.) Once you've eliminated the clearance, tighten the top.

The next step should be the primary, but before moving on, check the wiring. Check the voltage regulator, headlight wires, etc., and run them through their chosen route to the tube that they will be attached to. I use zip ties to have an idea and keep them in place (not fully tight, and with enough space for other wires to go through). Normally, the voltage regulator is at the front of the bike, and the preferred route for the wire is the left-side lower frame tube at the bottom.

Since we are installing the primary next, make a note of whether you're using an enclosed or open one. Remember that the primary is the piece that tells us where the tranny goes in reference to the motor.

Once the inner primary is in place and tightened, go ahead and install the belt/clutch combo. Check the manufacturer's recommended belt play, and then tighten the transmission nuts.

If you're going with an open primary without a backing plate (which is what we normally use), it gets a bit more complicated. If the transmission is from the starter era (1965 and up), you will need a bearing support plate. The tension on the primary belt will be very important since we do not have a plate. So first, you will need to install the belt and clutch hub/housing to figure out where the transmission will be tightened.

These transmissions allow for forward/backward adjustment. Since the old tin primary would not attach to the transmission at all, the plate has its adjuster. Don't fret if it's not there anymore; you can move it by hand.

Once you have the clearance on the belt correct (read the manual, but the key is to get it not too tight and not too loose), tighten the tranny nuts. OK, so now your transmission is set. Take the clutch hub and front pulley off, and apply some anti-seize compound to the shafts. I use a bit of red Loctite if I am using a splined shaft to reduce slapping and tighten the bond. If you need to move the transmission in order to fit the belt back in, mark where it was and make sure to retighten by the marks. Apply red Loctite to the motor and transmission shaft bolts (remember, the tranny is counter threaded), and tighten according to specs.

If you are checking off steps in your build, you have a lot done by now: the motor, transmission, primary, oil tank, rear fender and wheel, front end, etc. You may have noticed I am just giving the major components the spotlight here. For some of the minor parts, you will have to wing it. There are a lot of minimal parts that we tend to forget since it's just a basic bolt-on deal. Nonetheless, they are as important as anything else on the build.

Backtracking a bit here, and assuming you've already installed your carburetor/manifold, we use internal throttles on many of our bikes. It's a good way to clean those handlebars of clutter, but they are on the pricey side. If you are going to use an internal throttle, remember to drill the bars for the throttle cable. I tighten the bars where they will sit, tilted forward or back or in any position, and then mark were the hole will be. I do this for a very simple reason: If you just mark the bottom center and drill, when you tilt those bars forward, the cable will stick out from behind, facing you, and it looks like shit.

If you are using a normal throttle clamp, well, disregard most of what I said above.

The point here is that you can route that throttle cable the way you intend to (normally from underneath the gas tank right into the carb), and secure loosely with zip ties until you are sure it's the only component that will pass through that area.

ELECTRICAL SYSTEM

So now we can step into the realm of the dreaded electrical system. Although I do my own electrical systems on all of my bikes, and there are some things I will not disclose (or give a schematic for), I have figured out the simplest way to run the wires. (In all honesty, it was my dad's method.) Since our wiring is minimal, everything is essential but also very easy to troubleshoot. I like using one color for wire. I know it might sound weird, but that is the way it is.

You will have a switch (on/off), a three-position toggle switch (for the headlight), a 30-amp fuse, and a brake switch. That is the major hardware I use on my bikes when doing the electrical system. If you have a starter, I highly recommend using a three-position, marine-quality switch (Pollock makes the best one) with spring return (like cars). That way, your bike will start right at the key switch, hence avoiding buttons and more wires all over the place.

I mentioned I like to keep things clean and hide stuff whenever I can. Then again, everything needs to be reachable without much effort (or as little as possible). Here's a good example of what to do with a couple of coils and your voltage regulator:

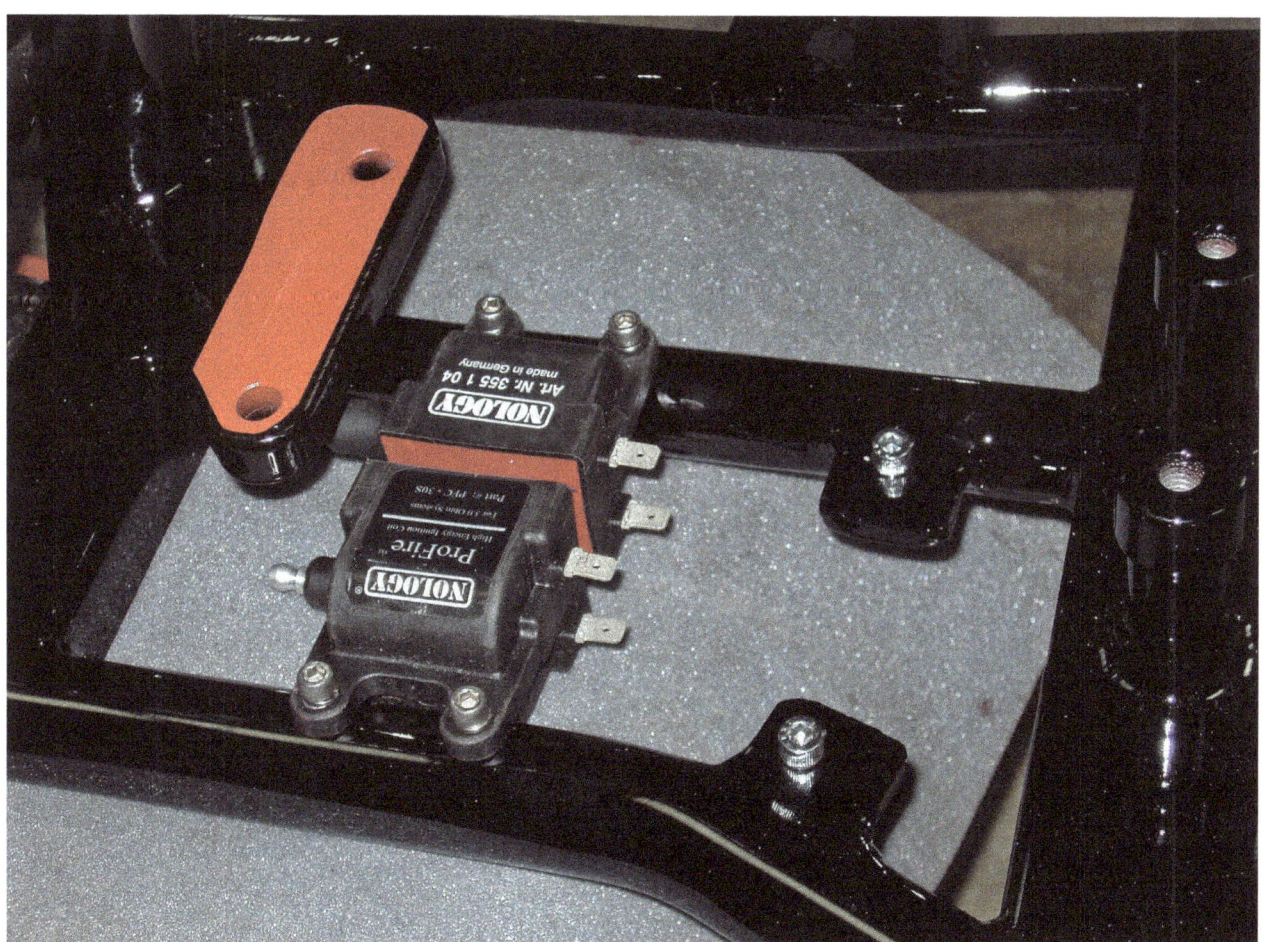

Of course, to get to this point a lot of preparation and pre-planning was needed. I used two Nology coils (since the bike is single fire). I always use these coils when using electronic ignition. They work great, and their size is perfect for what I like to do.

I also provide room for the voltage regulator. I don't know if Compufire still makes this model, but it is small and works great.

We try to keep the switch, toggle switch, and 30-amp fuse as close as possible, unless (and we do this often) we install the high/low toggle switch right on the headlight housing. Doing so will only bring a single wire back to the switch.

Our on/off switches are always close to the oil tank on the left side of the bike, so we tend to place the 30-amp fuse someplace nearby. If you have a battery tray on your oil tank, this is the perfect place for all the electronics to be placed. Another reason for the switch being there is that we can run the wires along the frame support post from the bottom of the transmission plate. Other wires that commonly run along that route are the ignition and brake switch wires, along with the voltage regulator.

All our wires are covered with heat-shrink sleeves. That's another little trick that will keep everything looking clean. Besides the heat-shrink sleeves, you will need wires and connectors, soldering iron, and a lot of patience to really get a clean look.

A good, clean, hidden electrical system that you can understand and fix yourself will add a lot to your finished bike. It's kind of an eye sore when you see a cool bike with wires and crap all over it. Be proud of your job, solder everything, and use heat-shrink rather than electrical tape. And if you don't get it right the first time, rip it out and start over. I've ripped off wiring simply because I didn't like the way it looked, or the routing, or that you could see too much.

You should hide the wires but not so well that it's a total pain in the ass to get to them if any work needs to be done. Remember that there will be a time when you will have to work on a certain part of the electrical system but not the whole system, so easy access will save you time and grief. As I mentioned above, a good part of being able to keep the wiring clean is having most major electrical components close to each other. The further apart they are, the further the wires will travel.

We use tiny batteries on our bikes. Since they are all kickstarts and have minimal wiring and lights, we don't need a very powerful battery. More cranking amps means a bigger battery, hence we can hide our battery from sight. One of my favorite spots to install it is under the transmission. Of course, you will have to fabricate the proper brackets, and the battery has to be sealed to keep battery acid off your freshly painted frame.

Just because you are building an old school bike does not mean your parts have to be from the Jurassic era. The best part of this chopper rage is the availability of good parts for our builds. Since we use smaller batteries that can be easily hidden, our battery wires also can be a much thinner gauge than normal cables and more flexible for easy routing.

As you might be aware, a bike's electrical system is a circuit. I have given you the major components of this system, and of course they all interconnect. Here's a short and simple explanation of what is what, and what goes where: The battery stores the power and will give power to the components. The 30-amp circuit breaker will serve as a breaker, so it will shut down in case something goes wrong in order to keep your electrical system from frying. The switch allows power to pass into the system. Your generator/stator will recharge the battery's power (voltage). And then there's your ignition, coil, lights (including the high/low switch), and the brake switch (sending power to the brake light).

There are several schematics available in service manuals. The only problem with those is that they include every single wire that a stock bike will use, and we do not use them all. I've found a few simplified schematics in different books, and you can find information online and in your local bike shop. Like I said, I have my own way of doing electrics, and you can find your own way, too.

ODDS AND ENDS

If the electrical system is done and checked, we can go ahead and place the gas tank. Since our tanks leave enough space between the motor, frame, and gas tank, we can work with the tank in position. Remember to add Loctite to the bolts and have a certain amount of rubber insulation between metal and metal, such as between the gas tank and bracket (it's not a must, but it does help). The fuel petcock should be installed before placing the gas tank on its mounts. Add Teflon tape or liquid Teflon to avoid leaks, and make sure the gas tank is straight before tightening the bolts.

Go back to the oil tank, making sure all the fittings are tight and facing the right direction, and tighten all the bolts. Add Teflon tape to fittings where necessary, and remember that your oil tank will already have all the electrical components attached to it. Once it's all tight, go ahead and install the oil lines. I do this a few times since I want to choose the best way to run them through where they're less visible, and very important, have no kinks or supertight spaces that might constrain the oil flow. In most oil tanks (custom ones), there are two holes at the top and two holes at the bottom, with the bottom hole larger than the other. The larger one is the drain plug. My bikes are meant to be simple, and the less shit the better, so my tanks do not have drain plugs.

The two top fittings will be either vents or returns and should be used as such by the line coming from the oil pump. The fitting at the bottom is the feed, running your oil into the motor. Oil lines should be 3/8 inch—not less. This will get the oil running smoothly without any obstruction or clogging. In case you are wondering how we make an oil change without a drain plug, we get the feed oil line off the pump and drain through there.

Some stock oil tanks have all the fittings at the bottom, and some are marked with their respective purpose. If, by any chance, they are not marked, there's an easy way to find out. Take the oil cap off, stick a flashlight into the fitting, and if you see light at the bottom, it's the feed. For the vent and return, you should be able to see the tubes going up into the oil tank—the longest is the vent, the shorter the return. There are many ways to figure this out, including putting some oil in the tank to show you right away where the feed fitting is located. I guess you have figured out by now how important it is to find the right oil connections; your motor depends on it.

Once this is done, we can tighten our clamps and zip tie the oil lines. Do not put in all of the oil yet. Just put in a quart, and check for leaks. If there are none, then add the rest according to the capacity of the oil tank. If you do find a leak, check the lines and fittings, and tighten them where needed.

CHAIN

Let's move on to the chain. We buy chain in the largest size possible. Harleys and such use 530 chains. Of course, by now, the wheel is in place with the caliper and spacers (spacers will vary in length depending on the frame and your caliper bracket). You should start by bringing the wheel as far forward as possible. Remember that the chain will stretch and keep on stretching.

A chain tool is another of those life-saving tools; breaking the chain and adding the master link is a breeze with this tool. If you don't have one or don't want to invest the money, then some grunt work and old-fashioned ingenuity will do the job. Remember that your new bike is not the only thing that uses a chain in the house (bicycles, chainsaw, lawn mower, etc.), so it's a good excuse to get the tool.

Place the chain over the rear sprocket, and roll it into the transmission sprocket. Apply some tension to it and measure. Remember that the links need to match in order for the master link to slip in. If it's way too tight, it will be very difficult to slide in the master link. Then again, don't allow it to be way too loose or you will have to go back later on and take another link off. (I do not like my wheel to go behind the center of the axle plate at maximum chain stretch. It could, but it would lose the contour with the fender radius.) Once you slide on the master link and tighten the axle adjusters, take a straightedge, and make sure that your chain is straight from the rear sprocket to the transmission sprocket. Turn the wheel forward, and watch the chain on the sprocket. The links should be about at the center line with the sprocket teeth.

Everything is in its place, as you might have noticed. All this goes under the transmission. The spark plug wires run from there, in between the motor and frame tubes, and come out through the heads. Also, check the wiring. Everything has shrink tubing and is as clean as it can be. I'm sort of picky about my work, but it's my work, and I take the utmost pride in it. Now we're ready for the transmission to go in place.

Double-check the rear wheel alignment using the axle adjusters so the wheel sits as straight as possible. Also check that the chain is not rubbing against any of your already-placed wires.

Now turn to the foot controls, forward controls, or floorboards. This is pretty simple—just bolt everything on. If you are using floorboards, bolt the plates first. On the brake side, you'll want to first install the master cylinder and then the brake pedal. (Depending on what you are using, there are instructions in your donor bike's manual. Follow them as closely as you can.)

Install the brake line from the master cylinder to the junction block (where the brake switch is) and the line from the block to the rear caliper. Remember to leave slack for the rear brake line since your caliper will move back as you adjust. Remember once more to add Teflon tape to the brake line fittings and the brake switch. Add some brake fluid to check for leaks, or in case someone dry pumps your brake lever. Add some more brake fluid, and pump the brake a few times, letting the air flow out and the brake fluid fill in. Fill the reservoir to the top, and close it off. Later, we will bleed the brakes after checking for leaks.

CLUTCH AND SHIFTER

So now we go to the clutch and shifter side. We have different ways to connect the shifter to the clutch. Some kits offer a rod with a heim joint, and it's a pretty straightforward installation. I've used chains, pieces of actual clutch cable, etc. Just so you know, this style of clutch is called a suicide clutch (there's no such thing as suicide shift). There's also what we know as a rocker clutch, where the rocker stays engaged or disengaged depending on how you press it. This style of clutch uses a rod, as well.

Since our clutch discs, separators, and everything else should be in place, our clutch arm (above the transmission top, in the case of older bikes) should have tension when pulled by hand. Once everything is installed, step on your new clutch a couple times to see how it works.

Since we are doing a foot clutch and we do not have the luxury of having a clutch cable adjuster, checking the position in which your clutch disengages is important. You have a center adjuster (no matter which clutch hub or manufacturer), and the normal way to adjust this is by bringing it all the way in and turning it back (loosening it) a half turn. Try your clutch pedal once more (on a hand clutch, you should have approximately 1/4 inch of play). Double-check and readjust all this once the bike is in running condition. For now, just let it be.

FINISHING TOUCHES

Remember that I have not talked about smaller components, such as coil, spark wires, etc. All motorcycles and builds will vary, so I am only giving an overview of the components that you will have to use. Also, parts are installed in different positions. You will be the judge of what needs to be done in order for the next step to be accomplished. For example, I place a lot of components under the transmission, so I have to install all these before doing anything else.

More or less, all that's left is the seat. Remember to install the springs into the seat first, as well as the seat bracket. Add Loctite to the bolts, and tighten the seat to the corresponding bungs. Last but not least, bolt on the exhaust. Loosely bolt the pipes to the heads and brackets, and tighten them as needed. I tend to tighten them slowly between heads and brackets, checking the seal between the pipe and head. Use a clean rag (I use wax) to clean the pipes of finger marks or any other stuff. Another good tip (if using chrome pipes) is spraying BBQ spray paint inside the pipes before installing them. That way they should last a bit longer before staining.

The front wheel should be tight by now, but give it a once over just to make sure, and double-check on greasing the axle, too.

CHAPTER 9
READY TO START

So your bike is assembled. No scratches, everything fits well, and the swearing and tool slamming was minimal. So let's get to it.

Our ignition should be in place and close to the correct timing. (If you are using points, get new points and a new condenser.) Please refer to the engine's manual for proper timing. It's time to turn the switch on and check for spark on the points. That can be achieved by lifting the points with a screwdriver and checking for the spark. You'll see it.

Test the headlight, both high and low beams. Also check the taillight to see if it's on. (We have not bled the brakes, so the brake light should not work yet.)

Make sure the oil tank is not leaking and is full. I kick start the bike a few times; that gets the oil circulation going and actually heading into the engine.

OK, so let's bleed the brakes. Fill the reservoir and start pumping. You need a buddy to help you out by opening the caliper valve for you. Also, double-check the caliper to see if it's aligned properly on the rotor (brake disc). Aligning the caliper will keep both pads (and pistons) at the same distance from the rotor and will prevent grinding later on. You can use thin washers or shims to align it properly.

A good tip, in order not to make a mess, is to buy a vacuum pump or simply get some fish tank plastic hose and a plastic bottle with a cap. Poke a hole in the cap so the hose fits through it, add some fluid to the bottle, and attach the other end to the bleeding valve. With this setup, when you open the valve, you will see the bubbles. In case you release the lever, all it will suck is liquid, not air, and you will avoid a mess. Once the brakes are bled, go back and check the brake light. Also double-check for leaks now that there's actually pressure on the brake lines.

Proceed to check your carburetor. The instructions should give you a guideline to begin with, an approximate setting so your bike can start. (You can fine tune it later.) Each carburetor gives you instructions on how to prepare it before starting. Also check that your throttle cable is opening the carb fully when totally engaged and that it releases quickly to the shut position.

Another tip: Have a fan close by to help cool the motor while you fine-tune it.

Pour some gasoline into the gas tank, open the petcock, and check the carburetor again. Look around for leaks and, while twisting the throttle, see if the accelerator pump is pumping gas into the throat.

Last but not least, get a spark plug and clip it to the cable. Hold it close to the heads, and have a buddy kick the bike over. You should see a solid blue spark grounding on the head. Try the other spark wire and repeat.

So now we have fuel and spark all over the bike. You have checked the three basic components that make the bike go: points, plugs, fuel. If everything is all right, you should be about ready to sweat your ass off kicking. And if you're one of the lucky few, the bike will start right away.

But, before we get way too eager, there's still work to be done. Get some tools, some Loctite, and a lot of patience, and check every single bolt and nut on the bike. Tighten those suckers (you will do this a few times again), and remember that those bolts are what keeps your bike together, so they are important. (Once the bike is started a few times, re-check the bolts.)

Check the fluids once more (oil, transmission oil, gas, brake, etc.), and make sure the caps are on their places and tight. Now it's time to *really* start the bike for the first time, we hope.

Make sure it's in neutral. Don't laugh. I've seen it so many times it's not funny (more so with starters). All kick bikes have a certain procedure to start. They all have their tricks. But here's an overall way of starting that kick bike for the first time: Give the bike a few more kicks with the switch in the off position. Since this is the first time we are starting our new build, you should kick it a few more times to get more oil into the engine. If the carburetor does not have an accelerator pump, use the choke and kick it a few times with the switch off. If it does, you can either use the choke or simply pump the throttle a couple times. This will get fuel into the chambers. If you have an older bike, retard the ignition a bit.

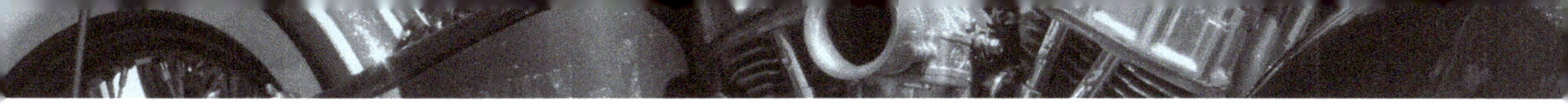

(In older bikes, you can move the ignition by hand. The left grip used to be the ignition advance/retard device.)

Kill the choke, turn the switch on, and turn the kicker until you have compression (until you feel resistance; there's not much use kicking on the easy stroke), and let it go. Repeat as often as needed until the bike sputters to life. Before celebrating with your friends, give some adjustment to the carb so it idles close to properly. Do not start revving the motor—just let it stay at a constant idle. Let the oil do its work and start flowing through the motor. If you take the oil cap off, you should see bubbles. That means that the oil is running—good job!

I do not allow new bikes (or refreshed motors) to run for too long. I'll give it a couple minutes and shut it off, then go back and do the same thing again. Even with a fan going in the shop, I do not like the engine to overheat. All those components are creating extreme heat, and they will settle down with time, but right now it's too much. Better safe than sorry.

So we start the bike again and again, until the carb is tuned right and it idles properly. If you can lift the bike's rear wheel, give it a once over through the gears to check the clutch and shifting.

I guess it's time to stand back, crack open your favorite beverage, and enjoy what you have just built. And don't forget to take a few good photos of your newly completed project

Photo by Frank Kaisler

READY TO START

The Journey Museum bob/chop. Photo by Michael Lichter

HIT THE ROAD

I had to add this to finish off the chapter. I highly recommend not going too far on your maiden voyage. If anything goes wrong, the farther away you are, the longer the push. Stay close to your shop or house, go around the block as many times as you want, but also stop and check everything on the bike. Give it a good visual inspection for leaks, loose bolts, etc.

If you feel something weird, stop and check it. I stop after a few rides, let the bike cool, check all the bolts, check the chain for stretching, and fix things if needed. I do this as many times as necessary, each time a little bit longer distance or more time. The whole purpose of this is troubleshooting, making your bike reliable and avoiding surprises while on the road. I assure you, there will be something. Just as I might be forgetting stuff while writing this book, so will you while building the bike. These are mechanical items, not magic, and stuff will happen. Preventive maintenance means everything when you are riding a motorcycle. I still check my bikes before a long ride, no matter how long ago they were built or how many miles they have. Bolts will loosen, chains will stretch, things will break, etc.

Enjoy your bike. Have fun, and be proud.

The Indian Larry tribute bike built for the Chop-Off competition. Photo by Michael Lichter

APPENDIX

Internet Links

www.ChopperFreak.com and www.myspace.com/elchopperfreak (Caribbean Custom Cycles, my shop)

www.LichterPhoto.com (Michael Lichter)

www.WestCoastChoppers.com (West Coast Choppers)

www.YoungChoppers.com (Hank Young)

www.TwistedChoppers.com (my brothers from South Dakota)

www.SugarBearChoppers.com (The Master)

www.ShamrockFabrication.com (Irish Rich)

www.Choppahead.com (Big Truth)

www.ChopperDaves.com (Chopper Dave)

www.FabKevin.com (Fabricator Kevin's steel parts)

www.CJS-engraving.com (CJ, master engraver)

www.ChicaCustoms.com (Chica)

www.Klockwerkcycle.com (Brian Klock)

www.Denverschoppers.com (Mondo)

www.StevensonsCycles.com (Stevenson's Cycles, Michigan)

www.SalinasBoys.com (Cole Foster)

www.CrazyHorsePainting.com (JoAnn Bortles)

www.DetBros.com (Detroit Brothers)

www.Motorcycler.com (Puerto Rican website and forum)

www.ZonaBiker.com (Colombian website and forum)

www.MotoRebelde.com (Venezuelan website and forum)

www.Kopteri.com (Finland's Chopper Magazine)

www.DiceMagazine.com (A great chopper/bobber magazine and site)

www.HawaiianChops.com (Hawaiian chopper magazine)

www.Bikernet.com (A great site with links to just about anything you'll ever need for your build)

www.ChopperTown.net (very cool films)

www.JBgrafix.com (Justin Barnes painting)

INDEX

Andrews, 68
Assembled bike
    First ride, 156
    Starting, 152–155
Assembly, final, getting started, 134–137
Avon, 14

Ballard, Duane, 118
Beugler, 131
Bling Cycles, 113
Bob's Back, 12, 15
Bobber
    Definition, 13–16
    Modern rebirth, 10, 12
Bortles, JoAnn, 122, 130
Build
    Financial concerns, 27–30
    Planning and preparation, 23–26

Caffeine, 125
Captain America, 14
Chain, final assembly, 149, 150
Chica, 10, 37, 117
Chop-Off motorcycle, 24, 31, 32, 52, 96, 113, 121, 125, 156
Chopper, definition, 13–16
Chopperweb, 46
Chris-Craft, 44
Clutch, final assembly, 150, 151
Compufire, 148
Cox, Paul, 31, 118
Craftsman, 38
Custom Chrome, 41, 43, 68, 78
Custom Cycle Engineering, 133

Daytona Rally, 10, 48
Devil in a Red Dress, 10
DeWalt, 35
Disassembly, overview, 100–103, 118

Easy Rider, 14
Electrical system, final assembly, 147–149
Engine
    Disassembly, 103–117
    Final assembly, 137–141
    Mockup, 79–82
    Tear down, 64–67
Exhaust brackets, mockup, 96, 97

Fabricator Kevin, 15, 23, 24, 110, 112–115, 117

Fender
    Boat trailer, 54
    Mockup, 88–91
    Mounting, 56–61
    Rear, 54
    Types, 61
Foot controls, mockup, 99
Frame, finding an inexpensive, 40
Front end
    Final assembly, 141–143
    Mockup, 82–87

Gas tank, 51–54
    Mockup, 88–91
Gaskets, disassembly, 117
Gennaro, 67
Goodson air cleaner, 67

HAMB, 46
Handy, 36
Harley-Davidson
    Big Twin, 22, 23, 29, 30
    Evolution, 21, 22, 30, 40, 65
    FL, 22, 32, 41
    FX, 41
    Knucklehead, 16, 22, 40
    Panhead, 10, 16, 17, 20, 22, 23, 40, 62–65, 129
    Shovelhead, 10, 11, 14–17, 19, 22, 23, 27, 31, 32, 40, 63
    Sportster, 17, 18, 21–24, 27, 29, 32, 40, 41, 51, 52, 87, 99, 101–103, 126
    XL, 12, 13
Hodge, Jay, 56
Horse Backstreet Back Talk, 46
Horse, The: Backstreet Choppers, 12
House of Kolor, 124, 129, 135

Imperial, 132
Indian Larry, 10, 13, 50, 52, 57, 96, 112, 125, 156

James, Jesse, 37, 59
JIMS, 37, 80
Journey Museum motorcycle, 10, 12, 14, 15, 20, 23, 30, 58, 91, 97, 113, 127, 133, 156
Knuckle Sandwich, 10

Lane
    Billy, 10, 25
    Warren, 10
Lichter, Michael, 12

Linkert, 44
Loctite, 75, 140–143, 145, 146, 149

Makita, 34, 35
Maldonado, Mike, 101
Mara Plating, 96
Misumi, 24
Mooneyes, 15, 46
Motor mounts
    Final assembly, 146, 147
    Mockup, 93–96
Motorcycle Mania, 37

Ñeco, 121
Ness, Arlen, 16, 131
Nology, 147
Norton, 22

Oil tank
    Final assembly, 144, 145
    Mockup, 92, 93

Paint
    Brand selection, 129
    Color selection, 124
    Design selection, 129, 130
    Preparation, 122, 123
Painter, choosing, 125, 128
Painting
    Techniques, 130, 131
    Tips, 131
Parts, finding inexpensive, 44–50
Paughco, 13, 41, 132
Pepo Paints, 102, 123, 125, 129
Perewitz, Dave, 131
Performance Machine, 15
Pollock, 147
PPG, 129
Primary mounts
    Final assembly, 146, 147
    Mockup, 93–96
Project motorcycles, selecting, 16–18, 20–22

Rear end, final assembly, 144, 145
Roosevelt Roads, 11
Ryan, "Irish Rich," 15

S&S
    L, 67
    Super B, 67
    Super E, 65, 67
Santee, 41, 43
SEM, 129
Shade Tree, 46
Sharpie, 39, 82, 87, 88, 99, 100
Shifter, final assembly, 150, 151
Sparto, 54
Sputhe, 68
Starting switch, mockup, 97–99
Sturgis Rally, 11, 13, 15
Style
    Frisco, 7, 13, 53
    Local Boys, 8, 12, 61
    Tuca, 9, 12

Tires, disassembly, 117, 118
Toggle switch, mockup, 97–99
Tools
    Advanced, 35, 36
    Basic, 33
    Everyday, 39, 40
    Expert, 37–39
    Intermediate, 34, 35
    Overview, 33
Transmission
    Disassembly, 103–117
    Final assembly, 137–141
    Mockup, 79–82
    Tear down, 68–77
Triumph, 22, 27, 54
Twisted Choppers, 52, 55, 91, 93

Unkle D, 128

Valspar, 129
Vasko, Johnny "Chop," 10
Wassel tank, 52
West Coast Choppers, 59
Wheels, disassembly, 117, 118

X-ACTO, 134, 136

Young, Hank, 10, 15, 44, 61, 101

Zodiac fabric, 10, 29

MOTORBOOKS WORKSHOP

The Best Tools for the Job.

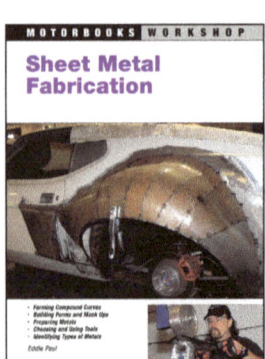   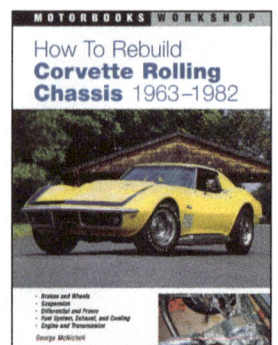 

Other Great Books in this Series

How to Paint Your Car
136261AP • 978-0-7603-1583-5

How To Paint Flames
137414AP • 978-0-7603-1824-9

How To Master Airbrush
Painting Techniques
140458AP • 978-0-7603-2399-1

How to Repair Your Car
139920AP • 978-0-7603-2273-4

How To Diagnose
and Repair Automotive
Electrical Systems
138716AP • 978-0-7603-2099-0

Chevrolet Small-Block
V-8 ID Guide
122728AP • 978-0-7603-0175-3

How to Restore and
Customize Auto
Upholstery and Interiors
138661AP • 978-0-7603-2043-3

Sheet Metal
Fabrication
144207AP • 978-0-7603-2794-4

101 Performance Projects For Your
BMW 3 Series 1982-2000
143386AP • 978-0-7603-2695-4

Honda CRF Performance Handbook
140448AP • 978-0-7603-2409-7

Autocross Performance Handbook
144201AP • 978-0-7603-2788-3

Mazda Miata MX-5
Find It. Fix It. Trick It.
144205AP • 978-0-7603-2792-0

Four-Wheeler's Bible
135120AP • 978-0-7603-1056-4

How to Build a Hot Rod
135773AP • 978-0-7603-1304-6

How To Restore Your Collector Car
128080AP • 978-0-7603-0592-8

101 Projects for Your
Corvette 1984-1996
136314AP • 978-0-7603-1461-6

How To Rebuild Corvette Rolling
Chassis 1963-1982
144467AP • 978-0-7603-3014-2

How To Restore Your Motorcycle
130002AP • 978-0-7603-0681-9

101 Sportbike
Performance Projects
135742AP • 978-0-7603-1331-2

How to Restore and Maintain You
Vespa Motorscooter
128936AP • 978-0-7603-0623-9

How To Build a Pro Streetbike
140440AP • 978-0-7603-2450-9

101 Harley-Davidson Evolution Pe
formance Projects
139849AP • 978-0-7603-2085-3

101 Harley-Davidson Twin Cam Pe
formance Projects
136265AP • 978-0-7603-1639-9

Harley-Davidson Sportster Perfor
mance Handbook,
3rd Edition
140293AP • 978-0-7603-2353-3

Motorcycle Electrical Systems Trou
bleshooting and Repair
144121AP • 978-0-7603-2716-6

Visit www.motorbooks.com or call 800-826-6600